JUST
another
HIDING
PLACE

DR SHARON ZAFFARESE-DIPPOLD

 ZeeT Publishing

Image Credits

Chapter 1- Another Unknown- ID 121453921 © Jbrown777| Dreamstime.com
Chapter 2-GingerBread house- Adobe Stock
Chapter 3- The Lock (Image by <a href="https://pixabay.com/users/skullman-914392/?utm_source=link-attribution&utm_medium=referral&utm_campaign=image&utm_content=801685">Ingela Skullman</a> from <a href="https://pixabay.com//?utm_source=link-attribution&utm_medium=referral&utm_campaign=image &utm_ content=801685">Pixabay</a>
Chapter 4- The Bedroom –(Public Domain)
Chapter 5- A Place of Darkness (ID 196148672 © Anda Mikelsone| Dreamstime.com
Chapter 6- Cornrows (ID 127738514-copyright-AndreyKekyalyaynen/Dreamstine.com
Chapter 7- Stars (Adobe Stock)
Chapter 8 – Patty (Photo 23024095 | Black Doll © Tatyana Gladskikh | Dreamstime.com)
Chapter 9- Closer (Shutterstock)
Chapter 10- Ice Cream (Shutterstock)
Chapter 11- Foster Family (Shutterstock)
Chapter 12- Another Car Ride (Adobe Stock)
Chapter 13- Garbage (Adobe Stock)
Chapter 14- An Old Castle- ID 196148672 © Anda Mikelsone | Dreamstime.com
Chapter 15 – A Chair (Adobe Stock)
Chapter 16- Please (Adobe Stock)
Chapter 17- Ever Again (Adobe Stock)
Chapter 18- Braids

www.GarbageBagLife.com

ZeeT Publishing

"Dr. Sharon Zaffarese-Dippold's remarkable journey as a foster child sheds light on the cruel and often harsh realities of the system. From turbulent waves to triumphant moments, her resilience is truly inspiring. Her story captures the innocence of a child caught in the whirlwind of life. You'll be celebrating her victories as she packs yet another season of life into that symbolic, black, garbage bag.

Blessings,
Ellen Torres, Executive Director
Casa of Hope, Inc.

Dear Reader-

I am grateful that you have purchased my book, Just Another Hiding Place, based on my true events of growing up in foster care. I aim to create awareness and advocate for change in the foster care system by sharing my life with you.

The past does not define us; you define you.

Living in foster care doesn't define us; we are worth more than mere garbage bags.

With deep appreciation and gratitude-
Dr. Sharon Zaffarese-Dippold

The author after making mudpies.

Content/Trigger Warning

If needed, please find below the following numbers for emotional support and guidance.

- ❖ National Suicide Hotline Number- ❖ 1-800-273-8255
- ❖ SAMHSA National Helpline for Mental Health-
- ❖ 1-800-662-HELP (4357)
- ❖ SAMHSA National Helpline for Substance Use-
- ❖ 1-800-662-HELP (4357)
- ❖ Mental Health- 211 (You can call this number for Mental
- ❖ Health assistance for yourself or if you are worried about ❖ someone else.
- ❖ 911- If you feel you are in a state of emergency, please call and someone to help you promptly.
- ❖ 988 Suicide Hotline

By sharing my true story about my experience in foster care, my goal as an author is to motivate and encourage you.

Remember to seek help if necessary and prioritize your well-being.

Your future is not determined by your past.

Appreciation

Thank you, Judi Fennell (www.formatting4u.com), for your beautiful cover creation, professional guidance, support, and top-notch editing. You offer guidance for every stage involved in publishing. You are the perfect combination of everything one could hope for. I am excited for you to portray the character of Anna in the audiobooks.

Kat Sheridan, from blurbwriter.com, The book's synopsis is incredibly powerful.

Amy Mullen, I appreciate you offering your assistance in reviewing the chapters as I continue to work on them. Your long-term help is greatly appreciated.

I am grateful to my Review Team for their support and guidance throughout the writing of Just Another Hiding Place. Your commitment, feedback, and motivation mean a lot to me.

Diane Rutkowski, Debra Holly Mosher, Melissa Wilcox, Bruce Sharpe, Gloria Thorpe, Lisa Marie Forte, Magin Clark, Melissa Lessord, Sherri Packard

My family, I am grateful for your support and guidance. Thank you all. I want to thank you all for understanding and supporting me while I was busy with the final stages of book publishing and couldn't take part in family events. You all mean so much to me. I love you!

Donation Recognition
Just Another Hiding Place
10% of all book sales

Casa of Hope
www.CasaOfHope.org

Casa of Hope

Casa of Hope is a certified 501(c) 3 nonprofit and anti-human trafficking agency for Survivors and by Survivors. We recognize fostered youth are 3 times more likely to be trafficked into adulthood and do not have resources to get out of entrapment to make a better life for themselves.

We are committed to remaining Survivor-led and Survivor-informed, making room for growth for every Survivor who enters our program to become a Survivor Leader in our nonprofit. Our mission is FIGHTING THE GOOD FIGHT AGAINST HUMAN TRAFFICKING.

With estimates of up to 65% of foster children being trafficked each year, we are dedicated to walking with Survivors every step of the way as they exit the life, providing hope and a future through emergency, safe housing support in an atmosphere of faith in Jesus Christ of Nazareth and in the beauty of holiness, according to the Apostles' doctrine.

Our passion is educating communities, outreach, and bringing awareness in an effort to combat modern-day slavery of men, women, youth, and children.

To send an offering of love to support victims of human trafficking at Casa of Hope, click on the link https://square.link/u/owrOtyzl, use the QR code below.

Storyline Details

This book draws inspiration from actual events. To protect the privacy of others, the author has altered names, locations, and family information.

The fourth installment of the Garbage Bag Life series, *Just Another Hiding Place*, portrays the language and thoughts of a child living in an abusive environment, resembling a nine/ten-year-old.

This book may not be suitable for younger readers because of the trauma experienced by the author, Dr. Sharon Zaffarese-Dippold.

To accurately portray Dr. Zaffarese-Dippold's home life, the author employed subtle language.

The child narrator in the book is not depicted on the cover; instead, there is a model.

Dedication

Mark Douglas Dippold

My husband, who's not just my partner in life, but also my unwavering supporter. I am constantly amazed by his strength, intelligence, and kindness. He walks this journey with me, smiling when I have to cancel date night for a writing night with no complaint.

This is dedicated to him.

Preface

Here we go again, a car ride to the unknown. I should be used to them by now,

But… I'm not.

How many more moves until I find that place that truly feels like home? And would my brother Curtis be there?

In my perfect home, I'd be surprised to see my brother sitting at the kitchen table when I walk into the new home with caring foster parents.

A creek will run through the horse pasture that surrounds the backyard. I swear I can smell the horse poop in my mind.

If my caseworker, Mrs. Alex, could take me to a place like this, it could help me like her a little.

I sigh.

It's only a dream.

In foster care, our dreams do not come true…

Chapter 1
Another Unknown

These rides suck. The woman driving this car, with her bright red lipstick, is as clueless as always and has no idea how much I hate being here with her.

I bury my head deeper into my brother's teddy bear as Mrs. Alex sings along with the radio. Her voice is horrible.

She's way more interested in listening to herself sing than asking me questions. She always tries to pretend like she cares, but it's all fake. If she cared, she would stop moving me all the time.

"Are you hungry? Shall we make a stop and have something to eat?"

And there it is—the plan to feed her ugly face that happens *every* time. Teddy's fur does little to muffle her rotten voice.

I bury my head deeper into his stomach, wishing Mrs. Alex would just go away.

Dolly, close your eyes and imagine yourself in your favorite hiding place.

I can hear Daddy's voice inside my head. Whenever I was scared of the dark, he would tell me to do that. But it has nothing to do with being afraid of the dark; it was my nasty foster brother, Derek, who scared the crap outta me. As soon as the lights went off, I always had the feeling he would hurt me.

But I guess that's not gonna happen since I don't live in that house anymore.

Mrs. Alex took me away. And away from my brother, too.

I close my eyelids tightly and repeat Daddy's words over and over in my mind. *Picture yourself hiding in your favorite place. Picture yourself in the hiding spot that makes you feel happy.*

So, I do.

The sluice pipe fort. I love that place.

The water runs over my feet before falling out the other side like a little waterfall. My fingers touch the metal pipe and trace the letters I'd carved into it—Sarah. It seems like forever since anyone has called me by that name. There's a big heart there, too. It says Dolly loves Daddy.

I remember when I made it and it makes me sad that I can't be with Daddy anymore.

Tears fill my eyes like a flood. Just as they are about to fall down my face, I remember hearing Curtis whistle near the stream.

"Anna? Anna? Are you gonna catch minnows with me or what?"

"Of course, I will. I'm coming."

I kick the water in the air as I walk toward the end of the sluice fort. There he is, my little brother, bent over with his cup in the creek, catching —

"Anna?"

I jerk my head up and see Mrs. Alex glaring at me in her rearview mirror.

Oh, no. I'm back to my nightmare. Ugh, how I want to return to my favorite hiding place. *Daddy, I miss you. Curtis, I miss you, too.*

"Anna, I've been calling your name multiple times."

Her yelling hurts my ears, so I stay quiet and try to cover them with the fur from my brother's bear. It doesn't work.

"Are you okay?"

Now she's whispering. This lady makes no sense. She yells at me one minute and then whispers the next. *Make up your damn mind, Mrs. Alex, and decide if you're going to yell at me or whisper.*

"What?" I ask. Why does she have to talk to me? I was in one of my favorite hiding places in my mind.

"You didn't answer me, Anna. Are you okay?"

She tries to be nice, but she's not. I know her game. "I'm fine, but I'm not hungry."

Will she ever get that these awful trips always make me lose my appetite? I wonder why, actually. I mean, my stomach feels like it's being stabbed, and I feel like I'm gonna throw up. But I don't. Probably because I don't have anything in my stomach *to* throw up.

I squeeze Teddy's big arms and lay my head on his chest while I look out the car window.

The trees, cars, and houses zoom by as if we're rocketing toward the moon. Are the people in the cars aware that I'm a foster kid? Do they know I'm alone? That I'm scared because I have no clue where I'm going? And do they know I always have to wonder who's gonna hurt me next? One of these times, someone may kill me. Do they know no one wants me and the only thing that big people like to do is hurt me? I'm just a kid. Do they know everyone ignores me, and no one asks me how I feel?

If anyone took the time to ask me, I'd tell them… I'd tell them… All the muscles in my face get tighter, and my jaw starts to hurt as I rub my teeth together.

I'd tell them I'm mad, sad, and afraid. Why does my life have to be like this? Why?

My legs start to shake. Holding Teddy tightly, I curl them up onto the seat. I touch the large swelling on my cheek from Mrs. Dorsey's punch. My eyes still look like a raccoon, so I'm sure this new family will think I'm uglier than Mrs. Alex.

Teddy's fur brushes my cheek as I press into him, trying to conceal the tears streaming down my face. When I'm older, I won't allow anyone to ever tell me what to do. No one at all.

Mrs. Alex lets out a booming, barking noise and then laughs hysterically like she's crazy as she continues to sing.

Isn't that what people do when they're happy? That's what my daddy would do when he was happy. He'd sing to the radio while in the garage. Is my caseworker happy because she is moving me? Ack. I hate her even more now, if that's possible. She took my daddy from me, my church from me, my Thunder, my foster sisters in the wolf pack, and my—

Curtis.

I sniff back a sob. I don't want her to hear me crying. I shift my legs. The leather squeaks every time I move.

Slowly, so Mrs. Alex doesn't hear me, I push my hands into all of the cracks between the seats. I bet Curtis left me a letter because the paper and crayons are still on the floor. I bet he did.

"What are you doing back there? Sit still, young lady. I'm driving, and I don't need you causing an accident. I can't focus on you and the road simultaneously, so sit still."

Simotanous... Simota... Whatever. Mrs. Alex must think she's smart using big words. Augh! She thinks she's so smart. She thinks I'm going to listen to her. She's stupider than I thought. I hate her, and don't care what she wants.

Oww! I jerk my hand back fast. There's something sharp inside one of the cracks. A big, red ball of blood pools on top of my middle finger. The same finger my foster brothers used to put up in the air at Mother when she would walk away from us.

Daddy's warning about it being a terrible thing to do made me never try it. I thought it was funny when my brothers did that to our mother after she yelled at them. She would have been furious if she caught them doing it, but they always waited 'til she walked away.

"We'll stop soon. The restaurant is right up here."

Crap. I have to check all the cracks fast before we stop.

I wipe the blood off my finger onto my pants. Then, being careful, I go back to the same place and thrust my hand into the crack again. A letter from Curtis isn't anywhere else in this car, so it has to be here.

I carefully inspect the back seat, making sure I don't overlook any area or crack. Yup, I've checked everywhere else already.

Slowly, I slide my hand between the seats and, once again, scrape against the jagged item. I push past it to see if Curtis tucked the letter deep inside the seat so Mrs. Alex wouldn't find it.

I press my finger against the sharp object, gritting my teeth even harder. The pain is like dynamite shooting up my arm.

I pause. I'm almost there; just a little bit further to go.

I clench my teeth harder, trying to prevent myself from sobbing like a baby, but it hurts like crazy. I try to keep my hand steady as I search for a piece of paper in the seat's cracks.

Seriously? Nothing at all? Can this be right? *Can* it be? Curtis forgot to leave me a note? Why? Curtis would've if he could've.

Carefully, I remove my hand from the seat crack. There's more blood on my finger, and some of it drips on the gross, leather car seat. My finger feels like a thousand needles are sticking into it all at once.

4

"Ouch." I can't keep my mouth closed another second.

Mrs. Alex shuts off the car and turns around to see what's happening. Her eyes widen like flying saucers. "What did you do? Hold on, I have a bandage in the glove compartment. Give me your finger." Her voice sounds hoarse like Mother's did after she smoked a cigarette.

Mrs. Alex holds my hand as she puts the bandage on. Yuck. I don't like this at all. I'd rather bleed to death than have her gross hand holding mine.

"There, good to go. It's bleeding a lot, but stitches aren't necessary."

My head jerks up. I cross my arms and scowl at her, pushing my teeth together. "No way am I getting stitches. Absolutely not."

"Relax, Anna. You don't need stitches. Let's not make a big deal out of this."

Mrs. Alex's door makes a squeaky sound as it opens. This car belongs in Daddy's junk pile behind his garage.

"Are you coming this time or not?"

"Not." I don't want to talk to her anymore, and that's not changing.

"Fine. Suit yourself, but the food here is good. Can I get you a burger or something to bring back?"

"Nope."

"Okay. I'll return shortly, and you'll regret not going in with me."

She slams the door, and the entire car shakes.

I peel the bandage off my finger and then fling it onto the car floor. This lady has nothing I want now or ever, not even a bandage.

Salty tears trickle down to my lips. Curtis didn't leave me a note. Has he already forgotten about me? It's only been a couple of months.

There's no chance that he would forget. No way. I bet that mean Mrs. Alex figured out our secret note passing, and she found the letter and threw it away so I couldn't see it.

Of course she did. She took him away from me, so throwing away a note is no big deal to her.

***

I hear metal scraping and glance up to see Mrs. Alex returning to the car with a bag.

"Well, how do you like that? We have the option to take food with us now. This is something I can eat while I'm driving. Are you certain you don't want any of my fries?"

5

She slams the door shut, and again, the car shakes.

"Has my brother been in your car lately?"

"Anna, you know I can't tell you that."

"No, actually, I don't know that. Was… my brother in this car? I have to know, so you gotta tell me."

Mrs. Alex breathes in deeply as though she's about to plunge into the water. As she turns around, I notice her staring at me with her eyebrows pushed together, making it seem like she only has one instead of two. Throughout my life, I've come across that angry look many times. She's furious right now, but I'm not worried. And I really don't care that she is. "Was my brother in this car?" Why does she keep looking at me?

"Fine. No, your brother hasn't been in the car. Let's get going."

Mrs. Alex eats a long French fry as she starts the car. The car sounds just as bad as it looks. If this vehicle had come to Daddy's shop when I lived there, I would've scratched it from the bumper to the fender.

I lean back and close my eyes, my head resting on Teddy's stomach. *Go to your favorite hiding place.* I'm back in the sluice pipe. Curtis and I are having a minnow-catching contest. I watch him count his catch, then—

Bam! I fly off the back seat, and I swear I almost hit the car's roof.

And Curtis is gone.

"Sorry, Anna. That was a huge pothole. It takes a long time to get to your new family. You will go to a different school and live in a new town. I think you'll like this home. You'll be the only kid living there." She stops looking in the small mirror as she focuses on driving, swerving to miss more gigantic holes in the road.

Teddy and I slide all over the rear seat. My butt slams into Raggedy, who's sitting up in the back seat with me as if she is looking out the window on the other side. My garbage bag keeps my old doll from falling onto the floor as Mrs. Alex's horrible driving gets worse.

I wrap my arm around Teddy's belly as I close my eyes to head back to my other world. But what will this new one be like? Will the kids at the new school be mean to me? Will the house be as fancy as Jessica's? Will the foster mother be like Mrs. Dorsey? Does it come with a garage for me to tinker in with cars? Could someone like Derek or Sue be living there and planning to hurt me? What? What is this world gonna be like?

My chest hurts from my heart beating like a drum, and I feel like I'm shaking all over. No one can answer my questions because my life is… it's just…

My tears fall into Teddy's fur. New worlds are scary when I don't know what to expect. Why won't these grown-ups leave me be? Moving all the time isn't helping. This hurts me so much.

I wipe my face and close my lips as I taste my tears. I squeeze my eyes shut as hard as I can and hold on tight to Teddy.

Jesus loves me. This I know, for the bible tells me so…

***

"Anna, wake up. We're here."

Slowly, I open my eyes. I wasn't sleeping, at least, I don't think I was. I was trying to get away from her.

I blink, and the car becomes clearer.

And so does Mrs. Alex. Ugh.

"Grab your bag, doll, and that teddy bear you're using for a pillow, and let's step out of the car. I have a tight schedule today." She turns back around and then opens her car door. She says this every time she moves me.

I think she's full of crap.

Mrs. Alex likes dumping me off on strangers and leaving as fast as she can. Today will be the same. She'll tell this new family all the bad things about me—then she'll stand up, pat my head, and tell me to be good. Then, just like that, she will be gone and not even care what happens to me.

Why would I ever tell her about any bad stuff? She would just move me, and who knows where I could end up? Derek had threatened that if I ever told anyone what he did to me, he would tell them to move me out of the house, and I would never see Daddy again.

"They will take you to a kids' jail, so keep your mouth shut." Derek had always snarled at me when he told me stuff. He'd looked like a dog with rabies.

But he was right about Daddy, so he must be right about the kids' jail. No way do I want to go to jail, so I will keep my mouth shut.

"Well? Are you coming, or are you going to sit there all day and daydream out the window? Move your legs, and let's get going." Mrs. Alex stands, holding my door open.

Daydream? She thinks this moving crap is a *dream* of mine? She has *got* to be kidding. Boy, this woman is absolutely crazy—that's what

7

my brothers used to say about Mother. They would say she was nuts when they got mad at her. Well, Mrs. Alex is nuts, too.

I'm not ready to move yet. I don't care about my new world or meeting any new people because I'm sure Mrs. Alex will just take them from me, anyway, at some point. So why should I care?

"Let's go, Anna. I'm not going to stand here all day. Get your butt moving."

The sun burns my eyes, but that doesn't stop me from looking up from the seat to glare at Mrs. Alex. "I know. I know you have other appointments and things you have to do. You know, you say that every time you take me on this car ride and dump me off at a stranger's house. I don't believe y—"

"Howdy, Mrs. Alex. Who de brought mey today?"

Then… I see her. A lady who looks like my wolf pack sister, Lizzy. She has the same pretty chocolate skin. Is *she* my new foster mother?

Chapter 2
Gingerbread House

"Let's go. Get out of the car now, and don't forget your bags."

Mrs. Alex reminds me of a raging grizzly bear.

I don't move. I scrunch my eyes closed to avoid looking at her and snuggle closer to Teddy.

"Anna, knock it off. Let's go. I don't have all day to wait for you."

Eww. Her bright red lipstick flashes in and out of sight as I open my eyes. I will *never* wear lipstick that color. Never.

With Teddy in my arms, I sit up carefully and grab my doll from the other end of the back seat—wait. How am I going to get my garbage bag?

I grab my doll's arm and slide her across the seat. "Sorry, but I need to squish you and Teddy together so I can get my garbage," I whisper to her.

Mrs. Alex holds the car door open while glaring at me. We find ourselves in the same staring contest as always. Neither of us talks to the other.

Do you think you could lend me a hand, you ol' bag? If only she could hear my thoughts, she would know how much I don't like her. Not that I'd let her help me anyway.

I hold on to the bag's top and pull with my free hand. Finally, I'm able to lift it up onto the back seat. *Phew*. The garbage bag is surprisingly heavy despite containing only the few clothes I have left.

I swear Mrs. Dorsey used to take our clothes from us when I lived there. The entire wolf pack would complain that we all had clothes missing. Lizzy told me that Mrs. Dorsey would sell our clothes to her friends for money. I wouldn't put it past her.

"Come on, let's get this going." Mrs. Alex's voice slices right through me.

I turn around and scowl at her. There will come a day when I'll seriously kick her.

I bend over, reach inside the vehicle, snatch the top of my bag, then pull it out.

It bumps against the car door with a loud "clunk."

"Careful with that door."

"What? Are you afraid my trash might damage your precious car? Really?" I yell. I can't help it.

At the same moment, both my doll and the bag hit the stone-covered driveway.

I hunch over to pick her up.

"Anna, don't be slow. Pick up your stuff and let's get a move on. How many times do I need to keep asking you?"

Ignoring Mrs. Alex, I grab a small rock and pick up my doll.

The stone's heavy, just like the ones Curtis and I would throw in the lake at Jessica's house.

I throw it with all my might, right at Mrs. Alex's knee—and now she has something to worry about beyond my garbage bag touching her car door.

"Anna, answer me."

I'm jolted out of my pretend mind by Mrs. Alex's voice. Sometimes, I think about things I want to say or do, but I do my best not to hurt people. Even Mrs. Alex. It wouldn't really do anything anyway. Well, except get me into more trouble.

I let go of the rock and stand up, clutching my doll and Teddy with my left arm.

Mrs. Alex is already walking away from me. "Please shut the car door, Anna, and come with me."

"Fine!" I yell. Using every muscle in my body, I shove it shut with a loud slam. The pile of junk shakes all over.

I turn and Mrs. Alex is standing directly behind me with a scowl on her face. She doesn't look happy at all. But I am.

"Easy on my car." Her mouth opens to say something else. I glare at her.

I wait for her next complaint about me when a new voice reaches my ears.

"She be a strong young lady."

There's no way that Mrs. Alex is saying that because she never says anything nice about me.

I stare at my caseworker, open-mouthed.

"Pick up your trash bag, and let's get moving," she says, snapping like a turtle.

How many times is she going to keep saying the same thing? "Grab your bag!" Ugh. This lady's annoying as crap.

"Hello, Mrs. Johnson. I've brought you a sweet young lady named Anna Snow."

Sweet young lady? I'm going to puke. It's disgusting how she pretends to be kind to me.

But instead, I glance up and see a small house. It looks kinda like the gingerbread houses we made in class right before Christmas. It's brown and looks like it's built with logs with small, square, crisscrossed windows on both sides of the front door and a pointy roof. The roof of the entire house has beautiful white lace. If we added some gumdrops, it would look good enough to eat. Wow. Maybe this won't be so bad after all.

"Where ya at, Ms. Anna Snow? Mey name is Mrs. Johnson."

My head snaps back down to see this old lady with curly gray hair. Her deep brown hand hangs in the air for me to shake.

I say nothing and do nothing because, even though she seems nice, I'm sure it's the same old thing as always. Even though she seems kind and caring now, no one can tell what will happen in the future. Plus, I can't understand her since all her words blend together.

"Anna, shake her hand and be nice. She asked how you are doing," Mrs. Alex snaps at me while she stands behind Mrs. Johnson.

My focus is entirely on the cool-looking house.

"None worries, *chère*. Aah not shake de strangers hand eider."

11

"You talk funny." I giggle.

"Y'ain't kiddin'. Aah grew up in Louisiana. Have ya ever heard of de place?"

"Nope."

"Y'all come t'learn mey talkin' better de longer we lives together."

Honestly, I can't understand a single word, and I hope that changes.

Her hand briefly touches mine as she grabs my trash bag.

"No. I got it." I forcefully snatch the bag from her and head towards the small porch.

Mrs. Johnson moves out of the way. "Sorry, *chère*, aah meant y'all no harm."

Sure, you don't. How do I know? You might hit me in the face, just like Mrs. Dorsey did. I wish I could tell this new lady what I'm thinking, but I keep my thoughts to myself because I can't trust anyone.

"Anna, why do you have to be such a brat? Mrs. Johnson is a wonderful person."

"No needin' fuss, Mrs. Alex. She don'tcha know mey, and I getting she wants t'carry de bags herself."

It looks like Mrs. Johnson is backing me up. Hmmm. Is she pretending to be nice because she's gonna want secret girl time? Maybe she'll force me to stay in an attic room. Or maybe she has a son who will hurt me like Derek did. What's gonna happen to me here?

Time will tell, I guess.

I tighten my grip on my bag and walk toward that front door that holds the secrets to what will happen to me in this new place. And Mrs. Alex is heading back to her car, not caring at all. I turn and watch her get her black bag out of the green monster vehicle. She leaves me standing next to this stranger.

"Let me getcha door for y'all." Mrs. Johnson smiles.

I'm scared. I don't want to be hurt anymore. What else can someone do to me that hasn't happened already? Is this the door to a nice house, a sad house, or an afraid house? Is this house going to hurt me? Why do I have to be a foster child going from door to door and never knowing who I will be living with or what they will do to me? If only I could run away. But… where would I go?

With my brother's bear in one hand, holding my doll, and my garbage bag in the other, I pause in the doorway. But I have no choice except to go inside.

"*Chère*, aah here t'help y'all." Mrs. Johnson's voice comes from behind me.

I fill my lungs with air and try to hold my breath for as long as possible. *Move your legs, Anna. You have nowhere else to run or anyone else who wants you.*

With that gentle—and sad, and scary—push, I walk into my new foster home.

As soon as I'm in the door, I'm shocked at what I see. This gingerbread house is missing a ceiling. I'm able to look at the highest point of the roof. This is so cool.

"It hurts de neck to look up, huh?" Mrs. Johnson stands beside me with her neck bent back, too. She is only slightly taller than me.

"Yeah."

"Let's kick things off so you and Anna can spend some quality time together, and then I'll make myself scarce." Mrs. Alex smiles out the side of her mouth as she heads to the couch.

"Leave de bag here." Mrs. Johnson points to the floor.

As I glance around, I can see every single thing—the kitchen counter, the living room, the TV, and the fireplace. All the walls look the same, like logs from trees.

My caseworker digs her papers out of her black bag, crinkling them. She acts the same way in every new foster home I go to.

Mrs. Johnson looks at me and points to the couch. "Wouldcha like t'sit down, Ms. Anna Snow?" Her voice is no louder than a whisper.

Nope. No way I'm sitting on the couch next to Mrs. Alex. It's not going to happen. Instead, I plop down on the floor and cross my legs.

"Let me give you Anna's story. It's a doozy, but important for you to know…"

Mrs. Alex's voice fades away as I look at the house made of logs. I already know what she's going to discuss. First, she'll tell her about my mother, Norma, and my sister, who had lice, and then all the foster homes that didn't want me. And, of course, how horrible I do in school.

"Child."

The soft, kind voice draws me in like a bee to honey. I turn my head slowly in the direction of my new foster mother's voice.

Bummer. She's sitting next to Mrs. Alex and is holding the papers, but Mrs. Johnson is focused on me instead of the papers. Then she stands up, drops them onto the couch, and walks toward me.

Uh oh. What's she gonna do? I keep my eyes on her and could probably catch some flies with my mouth hanging so far open. What the heck is this old lady doing?

Then… she sits on the floor next to me.

This is new— I gulp.

"Aah be's old lady, but aah can sit on de floor and cross mey legs like y'all." Mrs. Johnson stares at my face for a second.

Then I see it. Her hands are moving in my direction and only inches away from touching me.

I don't want anyone touching me!

Without thinking about it, I lean back.

Mrs. Johnson's hand freezes just like a statue's. After a second, she blinks and drops her hand. "What happened t' y'all pretty face?"

Mrs. Dorsey decked me, and that's why I'm here. That's why I had to leave my wolf pack sisters. That's *what happened.* But I don't say it; I just shrug.

"Anna had to be removed from the last foster home because she accused the foster mother of punching her in the face." Mrs. Alex pops back into the conversation with her scratchy voice.

"*Accused?*" Mrs. Johnson asks.

"Yes, accused. There hasn't been an investigation yet, though the school thinks it was one of the girls in the house, and Anna might be saying it was Mrs. Dorsey to protect the girls."

"You don't know what you're talking about." I dig my fingernails into my palms. "Mrs. Dorsey *did* do this to my face, you mean old lady." I feel like a race car driving a hundred miles an hour with no brakes.

I stand quickly and move in front of Mrs. Alex. "My wolf pack sisters would *never* do this to me. They tried to help me and gave me food when Mrs. Dorsey wouldn't." Crossing my arms, I stomp my feet. It's like drums echoing off the wooden floor. "How *dare* you say it's them and not that mean foster mother."

Mrs. Johnson jumps up like a rabbit and stands beside me.

"Aah hear y'all, *chère* I hear ya. Mrs. Alex, dis meeting is not helping Anna. It is makin' her head heat up faster den de pavement in N'awlins on a hot summer day. Aah got dis. Aah been a foster mom in N'awlins longer den y'all been a case manager. Aah fixin' we calls it a day."

I refuse to look away from my staring contest with Mrs. Alex. She has *no* shot at winning unless I end it.

14

She looks way older than Mrs. Johnson, who just said she'd been a foster mom longer than Mrs. Alex's been a caseworker, so that makes my foster mother older than Mrs. Alex.

I end the contest and turn my head to watch Mrs. Johnson. Yup. she looks younger.

Mrs. Alex clears her throat. "Allow me to share some information about her brother, Curtis."

That hits me like a knife in my stomach because she *knows* how much I miss my brother.

My legs wobble and stop holding me up. Everything in the room spins around me in a circle, going faster and faster until…

… there's nothing at all.

***

"Anna. wake up, child." Mrs. Johnson's voice sounds like it's above me. "What's this?"

Mrs. Johnson sounds frustrated as she talks with Mrs. Alex. I hope she's not upset with me. My body does this all by itself, and there's nothing I can do about it.

"When Anna gets upset, she passes out." Mrs. Alex sounds as cold as snow.

"And how de long has dis child been doin' dis? Don'tcha think we shoulda check it out?" Mrs. Johnson sounds concerned.

"Sure. I will make sure you have her insurance information so you can get her scheduled with a new doctor." Mrs. Alex speaks like it's no big deal. But that's not really a surprise because I know I'm no big deal to her.

Though I'm awake now, I pretend like I'm still out of it so I can listen to their conversation. Mrs. Johnson has my head in her hands.

"*Chère?*" She sounds worried and keeps calling me by the wrong name.

As I open my eyes, Mrs. Johnson's face blurs in and out of focus. Her dark brown eyes, similar to mine, immediately capture my attention as she looks at me.

"Y'all gave mey a fright?" Her fingers trace the hairline on my forehead.

Carefully, I sit up. Mrs. Alex is now standing with her black bag in her hand. "What did you say?" I ask my new foster mother.

15

"Aah ask… um… de word…" She looks up at the ceiling. "Aah ask if y'all okay?"

"Yes. I'm good. Now."

"Aah see dat a doctor checks dis child. Aah think now a good times t'leaves, Aah fetch de drinks for dis child whiles y'all sees yourself out of de house." My new foster mother stays fixed on Mrs. Alex for a second before she turns and looks at me.

"Anna, wouldcha like some sweet tea? Or, Aah made cha some Kool-Aid, as I knew y'all was comin'."

The front door closes with a loud bam.

Like every other time, Mrs. Alex leaves me with a stranger without a word.

"Kool-Aid, please." I can't help but smile at this kind old lady. For the moment, she seems like a nice person. It's possible that Mrs. Johnson will be kind like my old foster mother, Jessica. Those are the only two people who ever made Mrs. Alex leave the house for talking badly about me.

But I couldn't stay with Jessica after Mrs. Alex stole my brother from me. There were reminders of Curtis in every corner of that house, which made me feel both sad and angry. But Jessica—She and her husband were nice foster parents. It's possible that this lady will also be kind since she kicked Mrs. Alex out like Jessica did. It's possible, right?

"Here y'all go."

In front of me is a glass of blue liquid. I take a big gulp. "Mmm. This is good." I run my tongue around my lips to collect every last drop.

"Ga de don, I'm happy y'all like it." She sits down on the floor beside me once more.

"Mrs. Johnson?" I whisper while looking down at my cup. "I don't know what you said."

She giggles. "Aah sorry. I'm a fixin' y'all get use to mey talk in a short time. Ga de *don* means look at dat. Aah happy ya like de blue juice."

"Oh." I take another slurp. "This is good." I smile at her.

"*Chère*, did Mrs. Dorsey really do dat to y'all face?" Mrs. Johnson looks like she's going to cry. She reaches out to me.

I immediately jerk backward and close my eyes, expecting her to smack me—for what? I have no idea. Perhaps I wasn't paying enough attention and spilled the Kool-Aid while she was talking.

I brace myself, squeezing my eyes tighter as I anticipate the impending blow to my face.

"Child, yer body is shaking all over de place. I won'tcha hurt ya. Open yer eyes. Ya safe here."

I slowly open my eyes and find her looking at me, a tear sliding down her cheek.

"Y'all look scared like a hurt dog. I promise y'all be 'k here. But aah fixin' y'all heard dat many times before, huh?"

For a minute, we sit quietly, exchanging brief glances.

"Does dat hurt y'all still, child?"

I nod.

"I have de best thing to help with dat." Mrs. Johnson jumps up and walks quickly to the freezer in the kitchen. She pulls out something that looks like a pillow.

Who would've thought to store a small pillow there? I've never seen anything like this before, that's for sure.

As she gets closer to me, I hear a weird noise coming from the pillow-looking thing.

"Aah betcha dis helps. Put dat on de cheek." Mrs. Johnson hands me the little square bag.

"What's inside?" I toss it from hand to hand.

"Aah fixin' four square cloths, wid some rice and corn inside. Then, aah sewed it shut."

"Oh." I study the bag some more.

"Woulda like to learns t'make?" She points to the bag while tilting her head with a huge smile filled with white teeth.

I nod. "That sounds fun."

"Y'all hungry? Aah fry up some chicken?"

With Mrs. Johnson's help, I stand up from the floor. "Chicken?" My voice squeaks.

Her eyebrows raise on her forehead. "Yes, chicken. Y'all had chicken before, huh?"

Once again, I nod hesitantly. "But not in a little while. At Mrs. Dorsey's, all we got to eat was mac and cheese and hotdogs."

"Mac and cheese be good. Aah not a fan of de hotdogs. Tomorrow, we make groceries. Aah get de food y'all likes." Mrs. Johnson takes my empty glass as I follow her to the small kitchen.

Did she say that we were going to *make* groceries? I have no clue what she says most of the time, but making groceries is one thing I'm sure I heard right. I shrug and keep looking around.

This place has fewer cupboards compared to my old foster mom, Sue's house, but I like that it's smaller. I can see the entire downstairs. This way, I can always see what is happening so I know what to do in case I have to run away, or something.

***

"Yum. I've never tasted chicken this good before."

"I'm glad y'all like it. Aah learned from mey grandma growing up in N'awlins."

I'm too busy enjoying the delicious chicken to care about what N'awlins means. I can't help but constantly think about what my wolf pack sisters are eating tonight. Though, I guess I *don't* have to wonder because it's probably mac and cheese with hotdogs.

"Child." Mrs. Johnson puts a hand on my back. "Y'all look like ya head in space. And y'all looks sad. Do y'all wanna talk? Y'all done been through de more stuff at y'alls young age den most adults." I roll my shoulder backward, trying to jerk her hand off me.

When I look up from my plate, I see her smiling. If she expects me to cry, she's in for a surprise. I would never allow myself to cry in front of her or anyone else. Though, Mrs. Johnson *does* seem like a nice lady. Maybe I *can* share what I'm thinking with her.

But the other foster mothers seemed nice at first, too.

"Ahh, I'm okay. Your chicken is delicious, Mrs. Johnson."

As Mrs. Johnson sits down, the kitchen chair grates against the wooden floor. "*Chère?*"

I choose not to speak, assuming she'll continue talking. I swallow quickly and nod.

She puts her hand on mine.

As fast as lightning. I yank my hand out from under hers.

"Aah sorry. Does y'all not like anyone t'touch ya?"

Touch me? What does she mean by that? I didn't like how Derek and Sue touched me. I didn't like how Mrs. Dorsey touched me. The only person who I enjoyed touching me was Daddy and possibly Jessica. So, do I like people touching me? That depends if they will be nice or not. I'm not certain about this lady, so I have no idea what her touch will feel like.

"Nope. I don't like it when people touch me."

"Okay. Aah fixin' t'make sure keeps dat in mind." She smiles and then winks. "If y'all wants mey to touch y'all, just tells mey."

If I *want* her to touch me? *How* would she touch me? How do I *know* if I want her to touch me? *Why* or *what* would I tell her? I nod and smile at her, but I really have no idea what she's trying to say.

"Now dat we done take care of dat, we talk 'bout what y'all be calling mey." She looks down at the wooden floor. "Calling mey Mrs. Johnson sounds so… cold."

I'm confused about what she means when she says cold. That's her name, just like Mrs. Dorsey was Mrs. Dorsey. "Okay…?"

Mrs. Jonson puts her finger to her lip. "Mmmmm. How y'all dinks bout calling mey…" She stops talking for a second and looks down at her fuzzy brown slippers. "Momma Johnson?" She claps her hands together. "Yup dat sounds bedder. Momma Johnson. Whatcha dink bout dat?"

Her eyes find mine. I'm frozen with my fork in the air. *Momma?* She's asking me to call her Momma Johnson.

I jump at the loud *clank* of my fork hitting the plate. I say nothing and focus on the plate in front of me. I feel frozen, as if time has stopped around me—

Oh no, not another fainting spell!

But… it doesn't feel like it. My head isn't dizzy, and the room isn't spinning. It feels more like everything isn't real, like I'm looking at a picture of myself at the table.

Mrs. Johnson's voice, for the first time, sounds scratchy. "Is… Dat…" Her voice cracks. "Are ya… okay?"

I shrug.

Neither of us looks away.

"Um…" I can't get the words out.

"Aah don't like de kids to call mey Mrs. Johnson."

Her eyes droop like my old dog did when she was sad.

Is it really going to be hard for me to call her Momma Johnson? After all, it doesn't matter if I call her Momma Johnson or Mrs. Johnson because she's not my mother.

"Sure," I whisper.

"Great." She stands up fast and claps her hands together again. "Want a cookie? Aah done made chocolate chip, knowing y'all be comin' today."

She goes to the counter and takes the lid off a jar that looks like a woman with a red dress and a white apron. Just like that, the jar's head is lifted, and a cookie appears.

"I like your jar."

"Dis old ding. I got dis from my moder."

"Did your mother give you this gingerbread house?"

"Nah. I done bought dis house from de neighbor." She points around the house and then looks at me. "Didcha moder give y'all some dings?"

I stare at the floor like I used to do with Daddy when I had a hard time answering his questions. There are cracks in the beautiful wooden floor. "I've never really had a real mother before." Telling her this makes things seem worse. Like a math problem, it makes me even more sad, if that's possible.

Mrs. Johnson stands up next to me. "Aah sorry, *chère*. Not all moders make good mommies. Sometimes, de world does not give us whatcha want, so we do what we gotta to get from it what we wants." She stops talking and takes a deep breath.

"Aah sorry dis world didn't gives y'all a good moder. But it don't ya mean y'all not good for someone t'care bout y'all." Mrs. Johnson touches the end of my nose with her fingertip. "Make sure dat y'all gets in dis world what y'all want when y'all grow up." She winks again and then walks back to the counter.

If I didn't know better, I would say Daddy became a woman with beautiful, dark skin. Momma Johnson talks to me the same way he used to in my first foster home. My lips and my heart smile at the same time.

"Mrs. Johnson? I mean… Momma Johnson, does anyone else live here with you?"

Mrs. Alex has already told me that no other kids live here. But I don't trust her because she's done things before that I didn't know about. So, I have to ask for myself.

My foster mother puts her hand to her mouth, her eyes huge, as she puts the lid on the jar. "*Chère*, I done forgot 'bout mey manners. Aah failed to give y'all de tour of dis house and show y'all where de bedroom is. But before we do dat, aah answer de question. No. No one lives here wid mey except y'all now." She acts so happy. Her teeth are super white as she shows them all. "Come along. Y'all can leave de plate on de table, and aah be fixin' it later."

I follow her instructions. As I push the chair in, it scrapes against the floor. "I'm sorry, Momma Johnson; I didn't mean to scrape my chair against the floor." I stand feeling nervous, waiting for what is about to come. A scream, a push, a slap, or a punch.

"Dat Okay. Can'ts hurts dis hard floor."

"Should I get my garbage bag?"

"No, *chère*, leave it by de door. Let's see de house first. It won't take long, and you can deal wid y'all stuff later if y'all wanna. Aah shows y'all de bathroom. Follow mey."

Of all the things for her to say, she has to start there. Without realizing it, she stabbed me in the stomach with a knife, just like Mrs. Alex did by mentioning Curtis. I hate bathrooms, even in this cute gingerbread house.

Chapter 3
The Lock

"Here we are, *chère*. Not a big, not a small. Just right for what we gotta do in here." Momma Johnson turns the knob, then stops in the middle of opening the door to look at me for a second. A smile freezes on her face. It's like her mouth can't do anything else.

I'm confused as I stop walking towards the door. I don't see any reason to smile. There's absolutely none.

"Come in a here, *chère,* so I can shows y'all where everythin' is located."

Do I have to? Bathrooms always make my stomach hurt. And this one is no different.

Mrs. Johnson waves her hand in the air. "Comin'?"

I step through the doorway and get smacked in the face with the smell of pine as I move past Mrs. Johnson stepping into the room.

I spin in circles, looking all around. It's as if I'm surrounded by trees in the forest. It even smells like the woods at my first foster home. Tree logs decorate both the walls and ceiling. Mmmmm. The smell of trees. My favorite.

I squint as sunlight fills the small room through the tiny window by the toilet. The faucet drips into the sink.

Momma Johnson walks past me and toward the sink. "Aah been fixin' to take dis apart and find out why it keeps a drippin'." She turns the spigot harder, trying to get it to stop. She flings her long gray curls out of her face as she gets closer to the sink.

It keeps dripping.

"Well, *chère,* there's no fixin' it now. Let me show y'all de bedroom." She stands back up and walks past me again.

I turn around just as she is about to leave the room. "Um... I have to use the restroom."

My wolf pack sisters in my last foster home told me that I talked fancy. I guess I kind of did, compared to them. My old foster mother, Jessica, taught me how to use proper words. In her house, we didn't say we had to *go to the bathroom.* She told me to call it a restroom, which is a strange name for a room, especially because it's not a place I want to rest in.

"I'm fixin' to take care of dat sink later t'night. It don't madda right now. No need at all. Aah sure ya' needin' use of the toilette. Ida be in de hallway if ya be needin' anything."

I nod.

"Mais, Cher." Her voice is as quiet as a mouse's as she leaves, shutting the door with a click behind her.

Mais, chère? What the heck does that mean? What if I agree to something I don't want to do because this lady speaks a different language than me? I hear the door latch into place, so I know it's closed, but I have to check it for myself to know it's really shut. I just have to.

Like a cat getting ready to chase down a mouse, I tiptoe to reach the door. Momma Johnson mentioned she'd be in the hallway. I would rather not have her hear me, but I also don't want to make her feel like I don't trust her to stay out. But how can I trust someone I only met today? No, I can't trust her yet, no matter how nice she seems. I understand that she's an adult, and grown-ups hurting kids is something I am sure of. She acts like a nice lady, but so did other adults, but they weren't. Sometimes, people can act fake.

My ear throbs as I press it against the door. "Please, Mrs. Johnson, don't come through this door." My voice is so quiet that an ant couldn't hear me, so I know Momma Johnson can't, even if she's standing right outside the door. My eyes stay glued to the door handle, making sure it doesn't turn. Nothing happens except… I hear Momma Johnson's footsteps clunk down the hallway.

Phew. Finally, she's gone. It seems like she stood out there forever since I desperately must pee. Carefully, I run my fingers around the handle. I don't move my ear off the door as I trace around the knob, looking for a button to lock.

Where in the heck is the lock? I feel all over the door as my heart pounds harder and faster. There has to be *some* sort of lock here. My legs twist as I squeeze them together tighter because I can't pee if I can't lock this damn door.

Ugh. I take a step back so I can get a better look. Where in the world is the lock?

Oh, no—*there*. Above the handle is a gold-looking hook lock. The exact same one we had in the bathroom at—

I fall into the door, and the room starts spinning around me. That is the same hook that locked our bathroom door in my original foster home with Daddy. The same one Derek locked to prevent anyone from rescuing me.

The room spins faster, and the logwood disappears, changing into painted walls. The musty, old smoke smell replaces the clean scent of wood.

Wait. I recognize that smell. I'm familiar with those colors.

Every muscle in my body freezes, and the room fades in and out, over and over. I'm back in the bathroom with Derek. My nightmare has come true again.

How did I get here? How did I get here? Please, not again. Not again. Scorching water stings my skin like honeybees. *No! I'm in the bathtub, with Derek keeping an eye on me. He stands there, staring at me. Can't he just turn around? I know what he wants. Derek wants me to lie down on his bed so he can hurt my girl parts. I can't bear to have him just standing there. He's waiting for me to get the stinky shampoo out of my hair. I'll try sitting here without washing it out, hoping he'll lose interest and go away. My nose feels prickly from the hot water, my lungs quit working, and I'm unable to catch my breath. Derek's getting closer to me. I scream at him with all the power I have. Leave me alone! Don't touch me! Don't touch me!*

"Anna? Anna? Where y'all at? I hears y'all screaming. Anna?"

For a brief moment, I hear Momma Johnson's voice from the opposite end of the hallway. I've come back. I'm able to see the log restroom once again.

"Anna? Anna? Y'all 'k in der?" She knocks again.

I'm not able to speak or call out her name because my tongue feels paralyzed. Just as I try to yell, the logs fade away, and I'm back with Derek. He's kneeling next to the tub, ready to grab the washcloth from me. His nasty, sweaty smell makes my stomach heave. *Leave me alone! I'm splashing in the water, trying to avoid Derek's hands. Leave me alone!*

The bathroom door rattles against my head, and I find myself at Momma Johnson's again. My legs feel like jelly as I try to move them.

In slow motion, I manage to stand and turn toward the door, but the door gets further and further away as…

I fall backward.

Ouch! Pain shoots up my back as I land on the wooden floor. But the fall snaps me back to reality, and I'm no longer in the bathtub. I'm lying on the cold, wooden floor.

Momma Johnson's face is above me and seems to come out of nowhere. There are drops of sweat running down her forehead. She sits next to me, but I have no idea how she got here or how long she's been here.

"*Chère*, where y'all at? Why're y'all on de floor?" She lifts my head into her lap.

"Don'tcha move yet. Ain'tcha safe yet. Aah make sure ya 'k."

Momma Johnson is tracing the outline of my face. I don't like this feeling at all. I close my eyes, hoping she'll disappear.

It doesn't work. I freeze in place and hold my breath. Where else will she touch me on my body? What else will she do to me?

Please stop touching me. I wish Momma Johnson could hear what I'm thinking because I really don't like her touching me. As I wait, I'm nervous about her doing something that will not be good or will hurt me.

Then, I feel the warmth of Momma Johnson's breath near my cheek. Every muscle in my body goes stiff like a brick.

She whispers, "'S'okay, *chère*. S'okay. I won't hurtcha." Her fingers are still moving around my face. "I'm figurin' many peoples have hurtcha, *chère*. Y'all have nothin' t'worry 'bout wid a mcy."

Slowly, I open my eyes. Her lips are right up against my cheek.

She continues to whisper, "Y'all find that not happin' wid a mey. No, sir. S'not. Pas du tout." Her head moves from side to side as she talks.

I'm having a hard time understanding what she's saying. I think they're caring words because she has tears in her eyes that are ready to drop any minute.

"Where y'all at down here?"

"What?" She makes no sense.

"Where y'all at down here?" She hits the floor with her other hand.

"I fell."

"Aah heard y'all' screamin', 'Get away from me! Leave me alone!" I thought s'not okay in a here. So, aah opens de door, makin' sure y'all's 'k. Is y'all k?"

How do I tell her I don't understand her while lying on the floor in the room I hate the most in the house?

"*Chère*, y'all okay?"

"Um… Momma Johnson? My name is not *chère*, but Anna." I wonder if she gets confused because she's older.

She chuckles." Aah knows y'all name, Anna. *Chère* means you like somethin' or care about someone'. It's a N'awlins thing where I grew up in de bayou. Plus, aah fluent in de Louisiana French Creole and not so gooda English." She giggles.

"Oh. Oh, okay."

She helps me sit up. "Let's start slow. Don't ya move t'fast."

Momma Johnson is sitting behind me.

"Are y'all fixin' t'stand up?"

"Yeah."

"'K, *chère*. Let's get on up den." We stand together slowly. "Let's be careful. Don't ya want y'all to end up fallin' down again, right?" She squeezes my arm as she helps me up. "Y'all s'okay now, yeah? Aah not wantcha t'get hurt.

"I'm okay. Thank you."

She stands slowly, not taking her eyes off of me. I turn my head away from hers. Is she waiting for me to say something? Is that why she's acting like teachers do in class when they want you to answer a question? Well… I won't. I stand up but keep my head down and stare at the floor. Like always.

"Y'all 'k?" Her voice cracks.

"Yes, I am." I study the wood grain pattern on the flooring.

After about a minute of silence, Momma Johnson leaves the bathroom.

I cross my legs and walk to the door, closing it. I stare at the hanging hook and repeat the same thing over and over: *The bathtub is not where I am. I am not inside the tub. Derek can't harm me in this place. I'm safe.* Or at least I'm safe from Derek reaching me anyway.

Once again, I press my ear hard against the door, waiting to hear Momma Johnson's shoes click down the hallway.

Will she be mad if I lock the door? Will she hear me if I move the lever? Carefully, I grab the metal hook and slide it into the lock without making any noise. Then, as if I'm running a race, I make a sharp turn and rush to the toilet, keeping my knees pressed together. I'm totally clueless about how this could possibly stop pee from running down my legs, but thankfully, it always works for me.

Closing my eyes, I finally can go. I hate restrooms. And they're definitely *not* a place to hide—

Hiding place?

I open my eyes. Where am I going to hide? I have to find another hiding place.

Anna. You got this. You can protect yourself if you have to. If someone hurts you again, you're able to escape.

I know no one else is talking to me, but talking to myself makes me feel better. Like I'm not really alone.

Perhaps I'll go outside later and look around. How amazing would it be if there's a horse barn close by, like I had a few foster homes ago with Sue and Allen? My horse friend, Thunder, protected me from people—like the day Mrs. Alex showed up to move me. Thunder almost ran her over with me on his back. I wonder how my big horse friend is doing. I hope he's okay. I blink fast to stop my tears. I'm not going to cry because if I do, I may never stop. *I miss you, Thunder.*

I exhale. Every foster home is a new world to me, and that one is gone. Should I even bother getting close to people or trusting them, considering they will all disappear? Why even try? The closer I get, the more I will hurt when I can't see them anymore.

I'm alone now. There isn't a single person in the world who can help me. I close my eyes and exhale. *Jesus? Are you there? Just once, I'd really like it if you would answer me. Just once. Maybe I could hear your voice, and you would say, "Yes." A voice would be nice. But... I know you are there, so I am going to continue to talk with you anyway because I have nobody in this world but you. Please watch out for Curtis. I wish you could tell me how he's doing. I hope someone is being kind to him. Maybe he's in a nice foster home with people who love him. I'm keeping my fingers crossed. Well, Jesus, I'm in a new foster home again, but I bet you can see that already. This one seems nice, and Momma Johnson is kind. Hopefully it stays that way. And Jesus—*

Momma Johnson's shoes click on the floor.

Oh, no! She's coming back!

I leap off the toilet and pull up my pants while running back to the wood door.

"*Chère*? How d'ya do?"

"Um… good. I'll be right out."

"'K, *chère*. Just checkin'. I'll waits here in de hallway for y'all."

Oh, no. I forgot to wipe because I'd jumped off the toilet so fast and now my underwear is a little wet. I look around to make sure I haven't forgotten anything else. "I, um, have to wash my hands, then I'll be right out!" I yell through the door.

"'K, *chère*." Momma Johnson sounds so kind.

I raise my soapy hands to my nose, close my eyes, and smell the pretty scent. It reminds me of the flowers around my secret fort in my first foster home with Daddy.

"*Chère*, y'all needs any help?"

My eyes spring open. I forgot I was standing in front of a sink with running water. It's funny how a smell can take me back to an old place like that. I have a lot of old places where I used to live.

I was with Daddy 'til I was nine. Then I moved to Sue and Allen's. After I left them, I moved to Jessica's house. Then, I stayed with that mean Mrs. Dorsey. The only thing cool about her house was my wolf pack foster sisters. Now, I'm here with Momma Johnson.

Mrs. Alex told me I had moved six times before finally staying with Daddy. She said that when I was a baby, I lived with my hospital mom, Norma, for about a year and a half. Then Norma sold Curtis and me to my real father. I'm not sure I know what that means. But then he had to give us back to Norma. According to Mrs. Alex, Norma had been a great singer and went to Nashville to make a record. She left me and Curtis with Daddy. She didn't come back for six months. I bet she was busy singing and making all kinds of records and stuff. So, we moved back in

28

with Norma, and then mean Mrs. Alex said she'd had to save Curtis and me from our mother. I don't believe her. She just didn't like Norma and wanted to put Curtis and me in foster care—she even put us back in the house with Daddy. So, if I add them all up, I've moved nine times, and I'm only nine years old. How many times will I move by the time I'm eighteen and I can get away? I shake my head. Will I just get used to moving?

"*Chère?*" Her voice comes through the door. "Y'all 'k in der? Aah worried 'bout ya."

"Uh, yeah. I'm almost done washing my hands. I'll be right out." After I rinse, I turn the water off, but I musta turn the knob the wrong way because water flies all over my shirt. Why do I have to live with someone new again and learn the rules of the house and figure out how things work, like this darn sink? What if she hurts me? Mrs. Johnson could be like this pretty white sink. It looks all pretty and everything, but one wrong turn of the knob and everything changes. What happens when I make her mad? What will happen when I make a mistake? That will definitely happen when I start school. I take a deep breath and hold it as long as I can before I blow it out like I'm blowing up a balloon.

It doesn't matter, I guess. I shrug my shoulders as if that would make everything go away and be okay. Nobody gives a damn what happens to me. Besides, there's no one here to offer me any help anyway. I'll just have to do it myself like before.

I turn the handle the other way, and the water stops mostly. I dry my hands on the yellow towel hanging by the sink. The floor creaks as I walk across the room. What *if this lady isn't nice? What if she hurts me? Suppose she doesn't like me?* I can't get my mind to shut up and stop thinking about whether Mrs. Johnson is going to be nice or not. Does it really matter how much I ask these same questions over and over? The bottom line is that I'm about to find out.

Slowly, I open the door.

Momma Johnson's standing smack in front of me. "How d'ya like this?" She hands me a huge lollypop covered in all different colors.

"It looks good." I let go of the door handle and grab it.

"Let mey show y'all anoder room, 'k?" She takes a few steps away from the bathroom.

Show me what? Will I ever be able to make sense of what this kind lady is saying?

"Hopefully, y'all be likin' de room so y'all can make good a doe-doe," she says over her shoulder as she keeps walking.

I repeat what she just said in my head. I will what—in this room? Make a doe-doe? Is that like a doo-doo? Does she want me to use *another* room as a restroom? Thank goodness I didn't poop in that toilet since that other room I just left is for pee only. There are some weird rules in this house, but I guess I can deal with them as long as she doesn't hurt me.

We stop at a closed door. "There's a little *lagniappe* in here for ya. It'll make ya slap ya momma." Momma Johnson chuckles, and her whole body shakes.

She wants me to slap my momma? Is Norma in that room? Or maybe it's Mother. I could never slap Mother, no matter how much I might want to; she'd grab me and put my hands under hot water like she used to do. I'd rather *not* slap Mother and keep my hands safe.

I take a deep breath as I wait for her to open the door, my heartbeat sounding like I'm beating a drum.

"Here we are, *chère*." She's smiling so much that the corners of her mouth almost touch her eyes.

Why is she so happy about me slapping my mother and showing me the poop room? I'm never going to remember there are two rooms to use, and I know I will poop in the wrong one for sure.

And then what will she do to me?

Chapter 4
A Bedroom

"Whatcha think? Y'all like it?" Momma Johnson has a big smile when she opens the door, but she also looks like she's not breathing.

I look at the poop room… only…

It's a bedroom.

And I don't see a toilet.

Where does she want me to poop in this room? "I, um, like it. It's super nice."

"Yay, *chère*. Aah glad y'all like it."

I jump when she claps her hands together. Loud noises scare me when I'm not expecting them. Mrs. Johnson clapping her hands reminds me of when Derek used to crack the belt together in front of my face before he would beat me with it. I hate that sound.

"Aah so glad y'all like it. I wantcha to see dis place as y'all home." She taps my knee.

"Thank you. I feel like I'll be sleeping in the forest with all the tree logs in here." I giggle. "But where do you want me to poop in this room?"

Momma Johnson scrunches up her face. "Huh? I don't understand what y'all means? Poop in a here?" She tilts her head in my direction, and I can see the deep lines between her eyes get even deeper as she frowns. "*Chère*, I'm a confused. There's no toilette in dis room. This is y'all bedroom."

"You said that I had to make doe-doe in this room." I look at the floor again.

Momma Johnson giggles. "Aah fixin' y'all did hear mey say dat." She takes a deep breath. "I guess aah dink de same thing if aah herd someone say dat same thing to mey." She giggles some more. "Make doe-doe in my French Creole language means, y'all makes good sleep, *chère*."

"Thank goodness." I giggle now, too. "I was worried for a moment."

"Yes, *chère*. So glad y'all don't have to de poop in dis room." Momma Johnson joins in with my laughter, and before long, I fall backward onto the mattress, holding my stomach.

She lays back next to me, grabs my hand, and holds it.

Do I pull away? I already told her I don't like to be touched, but she keeps doing it. What should I do?

Just as I am about to pull my hand out of hers, Momma Johnson whispers, "I ain'tcha ever gonna hurt ya, *chère*." She lets go and then sits back up on the bench.

"Aah'll leave y'all to ya new room." Her voice sounds soft and kind. "Take yer time t'hang out in here. No rush." Her shoes shuffle across the floor as she closes the door behind her.

I stretch out my arms on the blanket. Aah. For the first time in a long time, I'm happy. I can't believe this is actually my room. It's completely different from my old, cold attic room I'd shared with my foster sisters. The paint on the walls had been peeling, and the carpet was dirty. There was even some of it missing. All our cots were lined up in a row, and there was only one small circle window. How fast things change from one world to the next.

But now... I look at a massive sliding door that opens onto a tiny porch off my room. This place is completely different. This room is... beautiful. And I'm so glad I don't have to poop in here.

I stand up and go over to the glass door. There is a forest beyond the backyard. Is that where she got the logs to build this house?

I tug the big silver handle to open the door. Oh, the cut grass smells so good. I have to go outside because I love that smell. It reminds me of when I rode on the lawnmower with my daddy. Maybe *that's* why this smells so good to me.

I close my eyes and hear the birds. They sing together like people used to do in my old church. I whistle along—maybe they'll include me. No matter what world I'm in, they all sound the same. Their singing makes me feel like I'm part of them. No matter what I've gone through and who has hurt me, I can still be free with them in the sky, or at least I can pretend to be.

And then I hear a horse neigh.

Oh my gosh—did Old Man Mike sell Thunder? Is he living in those trees? I shut my eyes again and stand like a statue, waiting for another call from Thunder.

I hear it again, a horse neigh. My eyes jolt open. Thunder? I dash to the edge of the platform and look around. I only see trees all around, and there is no sign of a horse. I feel sad, and my head has fallen onto my chest like a rock dropping to the ground. If only—

I hear it again.

My ears are right. With a burst of speed, I run to the end of the deck, then leap off the steps and head to the edge of the forest. There are all kinds of noises coming from inside that dark place, and the sun disappears in the middle of it. I have to talk myself into going in for sure because it looks scary.

Come on, Anna. You've been through far more terrifying things than this forest. Thunder could be in there! This is nothing to you. You aren't afraid of anything.

Right. I'm not. So, I run as fast as I can, my shoes crunching the leaves as I race over them.

And there it is—a big, beautiful, white horse behind a white fence. He's eating grass, so it probably wasn't the one neighing.

Sure enough, there's another neigh, and I see—

Holy cow—there's *another* horse, all black like my Thunder. And he's galloping around a pasture lined with tree logs. He's smaller than Thunder, but he's just as beautiful.

I pinch myself to make sure I'm not dreaming. I can't believe that I now live between two horse pastures!

I'm going to go see both of them!

"Hey, beautiful, strong horse. Will you come see me?" I lean into the white fence, trying to get closer to the huge animal. I smack my lips together, hoping this works.

Nope, it doesn't.

"Well, if you don't come see me today, I'll bring you a surprise tomorrow so you will. I better get going because my new foster mother doesn't know I left the house."

I run, filled with excitement that I have two horses living by me now. It can't get any better than this. I stop on the edge of the forest and look into the woods. It's filled with all kinds of noises. The leaves swirl around and bump into each other, and it sounds like small animals are running everywhere over the branches.

I did this once already; I can do it again.

Finally, I'm back to my small deck. I sit down on the pretty brown chair with a pillow that has "home" sewn into the fabric. Home? Is this going to be my forever home? Is there such a place for me? Why doesn't anyone want me? I strive to be good like Daddy taught me. I try to be nice. Well, that is, to everyone except for that mean Mrs. Dorsey who punched me in my face.

I reach up and lightly rub my cheek. I hope Momma Johnson won't hurt me like all the other foster mothers did, except for Jessica. She was cool until she let Mrs. Alex take Curtis away, that is.

The wind whips and a few long strands of hair strike me across my face. The short ones don't move much. My old foster sister cut my hair to be mean. So, I have some short pieces and long ones. I shrug. She turned out to be my friend in the end and one of my wolfpack sisters. I wonder how she's doing. All of a sudden, my head feels heavy. I wonder how all of them are.

All the people I have lost in my life just keep adding up. Every new world brings me new faces I will never see again when I leave. With a firm grip, I squeeze the home pillow. I always go away.

I stand and return to my new bedroom. I carefully close the giant glass door once inside. I'd hate to break something on my first day. It's then I see Jesus hanging on a cross on the wall. My eyes lock on it without blinking. *Poor Jesus.* As I reach out to touch the cross, I feel sad. Jesus has the nails in his hands and feet like I have in my heart, from people giving me away all the time and taking my brother from me. Carefully, my forefinger touches the nail on his feet.

If Jesus could rise from this and watch over everyone, then maybe…

so can I. I cautiously move my pointer finger over the body of Jesus. *I'm sorry people did this to you.* For a moment, I feel really sad. It's the first time I've ever had a cross in my room. I like it.

Knock

"Anna, are y'all hungry? Aah went and made some groceries." Momma Johnson says through my bedroom door.

She went and made groceries? How did she make groceries?

"Can aah come in?"

I guess I can't really say *no* since this *is* her house. But I like that she knocked and asked first. Other foster homes didn't do that. People just barged in without asking, like Derek, Mother, Sue, and, of course, the mean Mrs. Dorsey.

"Um, okay."

She walks in. "Aah made de some beignets and po' boys for y'all with some pralines."

Huh? I don't understand anything she just said. At least she hasn't gotten mad at me for asking questions, so I guess it's safe for me to ask some more.

"Um… Momma Johnson?" I turn and scrunch my face, looking at her standing in the doorway. "What's a beignet? And what's a po' boy?"

"Ah. Beignet is de homemade donut wid a some powder sugar on it. Po' boy is de sandwich on some homemade French bread like mey momma made in de bayou. The praline is soma good dessert." She licks her lips. "Yum. Aah dink y'all will like it."

I nod, wondering why a sandwich is called a po' boy.

"*Chère*? Does y'all know 'bout Jesus?" She nods at the cross that I'm still standing in front of.

"I sure do. He's my friend, and I met him at church at my first foster home."

"Wouldcha like t'go to de church wid a mey?" She keeps looking at the cross.

"Yes. Yes. I would *love* to do that with you!"

"Then we'll plan a trip to de church dis Sunday." She pats my back. "But if y'all don't eat somedin', der won't be much of y'all to take to de church." She laughs and walks out the door. "Hurry, *chère*."

I direct my attention back to Jesus. *Goodbye, Jesus. I'll talk with you again tonight. And thank you for bringing me to this gingerbread house with this nice lady and the horses. Thank you.*

***

As soon as I finish eating, I run outside to play. Momma Johnson insists I return before dark to avoid walking in the woods at night. She doesn't have to tell me twice. No way do I want to walk through there in the dark.

To reach the horses, I have to go through this dark place, so I run as fast as I can. When I am almost through the trees, I hear a branch snap. *Please don't be a bear!*

And then, at last, I'm free. I don't see the black horse in the pasture, so I decide to visit the white horse. It appears to be waiting for me, standing near the fence.

As I get closer and gaze at the beautiful stallion, I feel guilty and happy at the same time. On the one hand, a horse is my favorite animal in the entire world, and I can't wait to get to know this new one. However, the guilt I feel reminds me of Thunder, the horse I left behind. It makes me sad.

As I bend to move a rock so I can step on the fence, I feel something brush against my hair. I quickly look up to see a horse's nose right in my face.

"Hey you? Are you kissing my head or trying to eat me?" He moves its head up and down. "I have a surprise for you, but I have to climb this fence first to reach you, so you have to back away."

This beautiful animal doesn't listen and stands in front of me, his enormous head hanging over the fence as he watches me.

"It's nice to meet you two. Are you lonely being in this huge pastor all by yourself?"

He begins to run back and forth in front of me. "Well, do you want to be my friend? I want you to, and I think we'll be best friends." The solid white animal comes trotting over in my direction again.

"Show off!" I yell at him with a giggle. He looks so free like he could run away from anyone. I wish—I wish *I* could make my escape that easily. My chest feels like a rock is sitting on it. I sigh. If only I was old enough to get out of foster care so I could make my own decisions. If only I was free.

I better climb this fence to give this beautiful horse its apple.

The white fence's horizontal wooden planks form a perfect ladder, making it easy for me to climb and reach the top. I'm careful not to slip through the gaps between these not-so-big wooden pieces as I step from one to another.

Finally reaching the top, I pull the apple out of my sweater pocket.

"I'll call you Whitey till I learn your name. Are you going to come over here and get your treat?" The smacking noises I make with my mouth get his attention this time. He trots over to stand in front of me.

"It's nice to see you again. I'm new here, and I like it so far." I look down at the fence for a second. "Momma Jonson seems nice, but I don't really know her either since I just met her. But things can change the longer you live somewhere."

They *always* change.

"Here you are, boy. I hope you like the apple.

A shiver runs down my spine as the horse's soft lips tickle my skin as he takes the apple.

This horse has a good owner—its mane and tail are brushed out and free of knots. Old Man Mike, even though he was nice, was too old and scared of Thunder's angry behavior to care for him the right way.

The white horse moves his head closer to mine as if he wants to get a better look into my eyes. I stand still and don't move because I don't want to scare him away if he is trying to see if he can trust me to be his friend.

"What do you see, big boy? Can you see that I'm sad? Do you see that I'm afraid? Are you able to see that I wish I could be like you and run free?" I reach up and gently pet his nose.

This magnificent white horse jerks away from my hand and runs back and forth in front of me again as if he's trying to show off how perfect he is.

"Uh, huh. I see you. That's right. You keep prancing and show me how strong you are." The horse follows my voice and comes back to the fence as if he understands me. I extend my hand. "Sorry, I don't have any more apples for you. I'll ask Momma Johnson if I can bring you one tomorrow. I don't think she'll say no." He moves his head up and down, acting like he understands me. "You're hilarious Whitey."

"Well, hello, young lady. What are you doing feeding my horse?" A voice comes out of nowhere, and then someone is behind me.

I yank my hand away from the horse's mouth and almost fall off the fence.

After steadying myself, I leap down and see a gray-haired, old lady standing behind me wearing a cowboy hat. Her grin covers her entire face but doesn't show any teeth.

"I'm… um… sorry. I was—

"Well, spit it out." The smile is still on her face, but her words make me think she's getting upset with me.

"Um… I love your horse. He's beautiful."

"Yes, *she* is. Her name is Rose." With a limp, the lady heads toward the fence. The minute the old lady reaches the enclosure, the horse places its nose against her face. "Hello, beautiful Rose," she says with a cracked voice. "Did you make a new friend?" She kisses the horse's nose.

Rose. What a beautiful name for a horse and so much better than Whitey. As I glance at her, the lady looks at me; then, she points at the wooden post with a crack. "You wanna be careful standing on that fence like that." She walks over and then taps the spot. "I'd rather see you not get hurt." She pets Rose. "You can call me Ms. Nellie Inez. And, who might you be?"

"I'm Anna."

"Well, hello, Anna. I've never seen you around before. How did you get here?"

"I… um just moved in with Mrs. Johnson."

"I didn't know Mrs. Johnson had any kids." Ms. Nellie Inez sounds surprised. "Especially some white ones." Her eyes travel from my head to my feet.

I tilt my head. White ones? Oh. Momma Johnson is black, so I get why she asks. "I'm not her kid." I hate telling people I'm a foster kid. I should just tell her that I'm like the garbage that everyone throws out of their house at the end of the week.

Slowly, I take a deep breath. "I'm a foster kid."

Ms. Nellie Inez raises her cowboy hat while she stays fixed on my face. "Well, Mrs. Johnson is a fine woman who will be kind to you. We sold her that house many years ago. It used to be our ranch hand's house, but as the years went by, we sold most of the horses. So, there's no need to have help. Rose remains with us only because she is my granddaughter Zeta's horse." She turns away from me and pets Rose some more on the nose. "We miss our Zeta, don't we, Rose?" She sniffles.

"Your granddaughter's name is pretty."

"Thank you, child. It is an unusual name; my son and daughter-in-law like names from mythology. Zeta is the sixth letter in the Greek alphabet and means olive. It's also of Hebrew descent. And…"

Wow. This woman likes to tell me all kinds of information. I like to learn and find it cool that her granddaughter's name means something. But I don't have a clue what *descent* means or what Greek is.

"Um… what does Greek mean?"

Ms. Nellie Inez doesn't stop talking, so I nod like I do with my schoolteachers so they think I am listening when I'm not. I'm thinking about something else.

"I'm glad I met you," I say, realizing that I did like talking with her. Though, like my struggles with understanding Momma Johnson, I had a hard time understanding what she was talking about. "But I must get back to Mrs. Johnson before she misses me. Can I come and visit Rose again?"

"Sure, and maybe I'll see you out here. I'm sure Rose will enjoy spending time with a child again. Zeta lives far away and doesn't get to see her often."

"Thank you, Ms. Nellie Inez!" I yell before I reach the edge of the woods. I run as fast as I can on the path that runs through the forest until—

I trip on a fallen tree limb, lose my balance, and hit the ground. *Argh!* I stand up and pluck leaves from my hair.

What the heck did I just trip on? I'm sure it's a big branch or something. My knee begins to throb. I bet I cut it. I bend over to lift my jeans' pant leg to see how bad I hurt myself when something catches my attention. *What the heck is that?*

A shiny material is almost completely buried under the dirt and leaves. I push the leaves aside and see…

A door?

In the *ground*?

Chapter 5 A
Place of Darkness

I open it—I can't *not* open it.

It squeaks, reminding me of the spooky coffins from the vampire movies that I used to watch with my wolf pack.

The screech is scary. What if something dangerous is on the other side? Maybe I should walk away.

But I can't. This is something I have to do. I mean, what if there's something awesome down there? As I stare at the doorway, my heartbeat sounds so loud. It's like I can hear it in my ears. *What the heck am I doing standing in the middle of this forest about to open a door that goes, who knows where?*

I'm Anna. I'm not afraid of anything. I repeat over and over again. But my mind doesn't believe me as I think about all kinds of scary things that could be under it.

What if a wild creature jumps out at me? *Why the heck are you doing this, Anna?* I don't know what's going to happen, but I'm used to that feeling from moving around in foster care from one house to another.

I know you're brave, but this is crazy. I shake my head. *What if you fall? What if something grabs you?*

"Just do it, Anna, and get it over with," I yell out, knowing only the trees can hear me.

Just fling it open. I pull forcefully with all my strength, and—bam! The door crashes to the ground, and I stare into a black hole.

Maybe I shouldn't be doing this...

I *have* to know what's down there.

I inch closer for a better look. Somebody has fixed a metal ladder to the side of the dirt. I get on my hands and knees and peer in. The further down the ladder goes, the less visible it is. Carefully, I lean into the hole, gripping some tree roots.

"Hello? Is anyone down there?" My voice echoes back to me.

Then—nothing. What if something jumps out at me? I lay on the ground, peering into the dark hole. I wait and listen. Nothing happens.

I jump back up on my feet and move away from the hole.

I'll come back tomorrow after getting a flashlight from Momma Johnson. No way I'm going down into that thing right now because it's all dark, and I won't be able to see anything.

I walk back to my new discovery. The door slams closed, shaking the ground like an earthquake.

Mud stains parts of my blue jeans. I slap my pant legs hard, hoping to get the grime to jump off because I don't want Momma Johnson to ask questions if she sees that I'm dirty. Or get angry like Mother used to do.

I take a few steps but then stop. I should probably cover the door. I shouldn't tell Momma Johnson—I might need a secret hiding spot sometime. I sure could've used one from Derek.

***

"Thank you, Momma Johnson This po' boy is so good. And thank you for taking the onions out of it."

As she talks, she winks and smiles at me. "*Chère*, I won't put onions on de po' boy if y'all don't like de onions."

I'm not used to others caring about what I want and, instead, always forcing me to eat things I don't like. I've thrown up on the table a few times because foster parents serve me foods I hate, like liver and onions.

"*Chère*, aah beginnin' to dink y'all done gone forgot 'bout de dinner. Member, *chère*, I need ya back in de house before dark." She puts her hands on mine and gives it a little squeeze.

"Momma Johnson, thank you for giving me an apple to take to the horse. I love feeding horses."

"'Course. Just be careful in der pens."

"I met Ms. Nellie Inez."

Momma Johnson bursts into laughter. "Ms. Nellie Inez. She likes her entire name. But she a nice lady. Aah bought dis house from her after she done lost her husband in de car accident and she couldna work on de ranch. Sad, actually. She had a tough time wid 'er husband dying. She won'ta care 'bout y'all being der to visit de horse. But ya should be careful around de oder horse since it belong to de nasty girl called Cassie." Momma Johnson puckers her lips. "She de devil child, dat one."

Great. I live next to a mean girl. There's always one of them in every new world I visit. But I'm sure her horse isn't. I'll have to be sneaky and visit when she's not around.

Momma Johnson adds more sweet tea to our glasses. "*Chère?*"

"Yeah?"

"We need a talk 'bout de school. Tomorra, y'all shoulda go to de school." She takes a sip from her glass. "Are y'all ready for de school or do y'all want anoder day here before y'all go der?"

I don't have to think about this answer at all. "Can I wait another day?"

"I don'tcha t'see why not. Y'all just got here and needs a little time. No school tomorra. Done." Momma Johnson claps her hands together and giggles. "Now eat up, *chère*. Y'all needs meat on dose bones." She taps my shoulder as she stands to leave the table.

After I finish my delicious sandwich, Momma Johnson carries my plate to the sink. I can't believe she's really giving me permission to stay home from school tomorrow. This lady is super cool.

"Momma Johnson, can I visit the white horse tomorrow?"

"Aah don't see why not. Let's make sure y'all make good doe-doe tonight and eat a good breakfast first, dough."

"Okay, Dokey."

"Let mey cleans up and maybe we can watch a show together. I like de show bout de three men dat laugh and make a funny. Does ya wanna watch with mey?"

"That sounds fun."

She takes the last item off the table and begins singing and dancing as she races around the kitchen, cleaning everything up. Well, everything except the pan on the stove that keeps making popping sounds. I don't say anything since she doesn't seem to be worried about it.

This lady doesn't ask me to do anything to help her. I'm not used to people helping me as much as she is.

"Okay, *chère*, let's watch de show." She hands me a bowl of popcorn.

She chuckles at the TV. She laughs more than anyone I've ever met before. I hope this is real and she isn't acting fake. *Jesus, I pray that she's a kind and caring woman.*

She turns her head and locks onto me. "*Chère*, aah dink de time for y'all t'go make good doe-doe." She reaches over and rubs my arm.

Her urging me to make doe-doe is something I may never get used to. I can't stop myself from laughing and grabbing my stomach.

Momma Johnson joins me while we stand up from the sofa, and she follows me down the hallway.

"*Chère*, I have new brushes for ya teeth in de sink drawer wid a toothpaste. Also, aah left de cloth to wipe y'all face before y'all make doe-doe. Aah wait for y'all in de bedroom."

As I head toward the bathroom, Momma Johnson moves past me but stops quickly to face me. "Aah forgot. Aah left y'all some pyjimis. Aah hopes de fit."

"Um, what did you say?"

"Aah left y'all some… pa… jamas." She stutters when finding the English word.

"Okay, thank you."

Why is it important to wash my face before I go to bed? That's something new. It seems like I discover all kinds of new things in every foster home I stay in. I guess that is a good thing.

Momma Johnson is sitting on the edge of the beautiful bed, with the blankets neatly folded, all of a sudden, my heart beats fast.

Please don't let this be secret girl time like with Sue, my old foster mother.

It looks like Momma Johnson turned to Sue's naked body, sitting on the side of the bed with her fingers stroking the blanket for me to join her. I come to a stop at the foot of the bed. I can no longer move my legs. My arms aren't working either.

Then I see Sue's mouth moving, but I can't hear any words. Everything around me turns fuzzy.

"An—"

As I sink further down in the water, I find it hard to breathe. I picture myself floating as the sunlight dances off the top of the water. The voice that always tries to help me is saying, "Swim, Anna. Swim." Sometimes, it brings back memories of my foster daddy, and other times, I'm convinced it's Jesus speaking to me. Trying to save me.

"Anna, wake up." Opening my eyes, I discover my face covered in something wet and cold.

"*Chère*, y'all done gave me fright. We need t'go t'de doctor to find out why ya keep a doing dis, c*hère*." She rubs my cheek softly.

"Yes?" I whisper as the room around me comes into focus.

Momma Johnson sits beside me, placing a cold washcloth on my face. "What happen, *chère*? What scare ya?"

How did she realize that I was afraid? "Sue was on my bed." I can barely hear my voice, so I'm not sure she heard me.

With the icy cloth, she continues to brush my skin. "*Chère*, who's Sue? No one here but mey." She lays her hand on my head and strokes my hair as if she's trying to make it flat.

"I thought I saw Sue sitting on the edge of the bed," I mumble, my voice cracking, "I truly thought she was here."

"Let's get ya sittin' up." Momma Johnson helps me get into a seated position on the floor. "*Chère*, who's Sue? And did ya get hurt by dis lady?" She leans closer.

Oh, shoot. I gave away more than I should have. I want to make sure this lady doesn't have a bad view of me. I simply can't bring myself to tell her about Sue. Just as Derek mentioned in my first foster home, she'll think I'm dirty.

"She's no one. In my previous foster home, I had a foster sister named Sue, who would constantly pick on me while we shared a bedroom." *Phew.* I came up with that lie quick. Please let her buy it so I don't have to talk about Sue anymore. It makes my stomach hurt like someone punched me.

Momma Johnson brings her eyebrows together. "All right, *chère*, let's stand up slowly and make y'all way to de bed," she says after taking a big breath.

"How did Raggedy and Teddy get on my bed? I didn't put them there."

"Aah did dat for y'all and aah put de clothes in de dresser. Y'all didn't have dat much, so I done and bought y'all some more." She smiles at me again. "Dey all in de dresser." She points to the pajamas I'm wearing. "Does dey fit good?"

"Yes, thank you. They're very soft."

"Slide in, *chère*, and aah pull de covers over y'all."

I do as she asks.

"Der, ya go. Now make good doe-doe."

"I will, thank you." I pat the blanket around me. Maybe I can sleep well. It's been a long time since I could do that with Derek, Sue, or Mrs. Dorsey.

"Did I do a somedin', *chère*, dat scared y'all? Y'all can talk to de mey 'bout anythin'. I won't ever hurt ya, *chère*." She tucks the blanket around my neck and rubs my head. "Do y'all feel de bedder? Does y'all needs mey to stay in de room wid ya?"

"No, Momma Johnson. I'm feeling fine and ready to go to sleep."

She softly pats the blanket that covers my arm.

"Okay, den. Don't ya forget y'all prayers to Jesus before y'all close dose eyes, *chère*. Night and aah see ya in de mornin'." With that, Momma Johnson walks out of the room.

I lay staring at the door. *Could I really sleep and not worry?* Maybe I should get up and put something in front of the door so if she moves it, the noise will wake me up. I toss and turn.

Quietly, I step onto the wood floor and walk to the wooden chair sitting against the wall with a blanket on it.

This will work perfectly. I set it down in front of the door. I will definitely hear this move if someone tries to come into my room.

***

A knock on the door wakes me. "Mornin', *chère*. Breakfast is a on de table." I sit up fast and see the chair in the same spot I left it last night. I take a deep breath and let it out slowly. The smell of bacon and coffee fills the house.

"What's a der plans for de day?" Momma Johnson plops grits on my plate.

"Um. I... wanted to... um... visit the white horse." I look down at my plate. I hope she doesn't tell me no. I hate asking people to do things because I hate hearing the word no.

45

"How 'bout after de lunch. Aah gotta make groceries, and I can ask Ms. Nellie Inez to keep an ear out for ya. Dat 'k wid ya?" She takes a bite of her pancake.

"Thank you. I like Ms. Nellie Inez. She likes to tell me all kinds of things."

"She sure does. She a nice lady."

"Momma Johnson?" I still feel nervous asking questions. I shouldn't, though, because she doesn't get mad when I do.

"Can I call you Momma Jay rather than Momma Johnson?"

Her fork falls onto the plate. She pauses for a second and then grabs my hand. I think she forgot that I asked her to stop touching me. But I don't want to hurt her feelings by asking her to stop because she's been super nice so far.

So, I don't say anything.

"Aah loves dat *chère*. Momma Jay sounds nice." She gives my hand a squeeze.

"Can I ask you something else?" She nods.

"Horses love apples. Could I take the white horse an apple today?"

"Sure ya can. Ya can find dem in de drawer in the bottom of de fridge. Help ya self."

"Thank you." I jump up and down in my seat.

"Now what else does ya likes t'eat? Aah make sure t'pick it up a de store."

I don't need to think about my answer long. "Peanut butter and jelly and cereal are my favorite things. I don't like liver, vegetables, or cabbage and ham." For a moment, I swear I can gag on the memory of Mother making me sit at the table and eat my entire plate.

"Aah make sures I only make what ya likes t'eat den."

Amazing. So far, I like everything about living here.

"Wells, I bedder move it along. Aah gots works t'do in dis house." She stands and begins to clear the table.

"Can I help do something?"

"Nah, *chère*. Ya be a kid and do somethin' ya likes t'do." The dish clangs in the sink as she plops it in to wash them.

"I like to help. Can I clear the table and wash it for you? I don't mind. I'd like to help you." She turns from the sink and looks at everything still on the table from breakfast.

"Okay, den. dank ya, *chère*. Ya can help mey wid de table. But let mey turn on some music."

I have no idea what the words to the song playing on the radio are, but that doesn't stop me from spinning in circles and dancing with the milk container as I take it to the fridge. Who knew that cleaning could be so much fun?

The morning went fast as Momma Jay and I finished cleaning the living room. She gave me a cloth and spray so I could clean all the wood. She calls it dusting.

"Are ya ready for a sandwich so ya can go visit de horse? Ms. Nellie Inez is working outside and she done said she'd check in on ya. But if ya needs anythin', you can go to her house. Dat 'k wid ya?

"Yes, I'm good with that."

I take the last bite of my sandwich as I stand up to grab the apple from the fridge.

"No goin' out front. Ya can play in de woods or by de house of Ms. Nellie Inez.

"I will." With my apple in hand, I head out the back door as Momma Jay leaves out the front.

I toss the apple in the air as I stand on the edge of my deck. Yup, Rose will enjoy this.

Crap. I forgot the flashlight. I walk to the corner of the house and see Momma Jay leave the driveway.

I didn't want to ask her about the flashlight as I didn't know if I could lie to her about why I wanted it. I don't think she'd let me go inside a dark cave.

I pull out all the drawers in the kitchen until I find the light and then slide it into my sweater pocket.

Like all the times before, I stop on the edge of the woods and build up enough courage to enter.

All right, forest, I've got my light, so you can't scare me now.

I will check out the secret door first before I feed Rose the apple.

The cold handle sends chills up my arm and through my whole body once again, making goosebumps stand up everywhere. It's as if the coldness of the handle is warning me about the danger lurking under the door. With a lot of effort, I lift it anyway.

Whoa! I gaze into the dark opening. Carefully. I place the apple into my pocket and grab the flashlight from my jeans. The hole pulls at me like a magnet that wants to drag me to its bottom. It wants me to explore it.

The glow shows me dirt at the bottom of the ladder on the wall when

I point the light into the dark hole. I am *not* going to be scared. Even if there are snakes down there, I'll be okay because I'm used to picking them up by the head.

I pick up a long stick from the ground and hurl it into the hole—a branch can be a helpful tool for grabbing snakes. Especially bright-colored ones that are poisonous or perhaps a rattlesnake. Now, I'm set to face whatever lies down there.

I take a moment halfway down the ladder to get a good look around. It's so shadowy down here that it's hard to see anything. I shift the flashlight around and can tell it's a small room with no signs of any animals.

Hmm, there really isn't anything to be afraid of after all.

This room is actually bigger than it looked from the ladder. There's also a tunnel. *Wonder where it goes...* I can't see anything in the tunnel from here, but I'm going to check that out.

My sneakers hit a big rock as I step off the wiggly ladder. I give it a shake. I'm putting my trust in this thing to hold my weight when I climb it to leave.

"Hi, Snakes. Hi, Bugs. Hey, tiny creepy crawlers. You have no need to worry about me. I just want to see what your home looks like!" I yell out just in case they're hiding from me somewhere.

The ground in the tunnel goes down a little. As I bend over, the apple falls out of my pocket.

Darn it. I have to get the apple for Rose. I draw a deep breath and shine the flashlight into the darkness. I take a step, then another, and another. The tunnel gets smaller, so I have to duck my head so that I don't get any of the dirt ceiling in my hair.

This tunnel reminds me of the small ones I used to make into the dirt bank behind my first foster home. I used to crawl into them to hide from my brother because he was too chicken to come in after me. But this—

I rub the dirt wall. Somebody really worked hard on this one because a grown-up could fit in here. I wonder where it goes.

It's so quiet I can't hear anything at all. Not even the forest. This hiding place is absolutely perfect, unlike any I've had before. Nobody would be able to find me inside here. It's not like my hiding spot with Thunder and his barn. No one knew I'd go visit him every night. But somehow. Mrs. Alex was able to find me the day she came to take me away. No way she'd find this one.

The glow from my flashlight flickers. Then… it's off. *Oh, no!*

The room goes dark. I wiggle the flashlight in my hands fast, trying to get some light, but I don't move because I can't see anything.

"Come on, you darn thing—work!" I yell at the stupid light. The glow comes on, though it's not as bright.

It's at that moment I see something behind the apple.

I freeze. What in the world is that? My knees shake uncontrollably, just like they always do when I'm terrified. I lean forward without stepping, trying to get a better look. It seems like there's a…

Kid? Is that a kid sitting in the tunnel?

In the dark tunnel.

Alone.

Darn it—someone else has already found this place. I guess I should be nice to whoever it is so they will share their spot with me and not tell anyone else about it.

"Hello?" I can't see him or her all that clearly; I can only make out a shadow. "I'm Anna, and I'm new here."

Nothing. The kid doesn't move.

My flashlight gets dimmer again. I need to get out of here, so I don't end up in the dark again.

But the kid is right there. And if he or she isn't able to talk, maybe I should see if I can help.

I head toward them, but they still don't move.

I shine the little light I have left in their direction.

It's not a kid—it's a… baby doll?

It's a very old, black baby doll leaning up against the dirt wall. Her eyes are made of black buttons, and her hair looks like yarn, but—not. There's a tiny, red line running straight across her face. She isn't as tall as my doll, but she's close.

I point my flashlight at her, then set it on the ground so I can touch her and still see what I'm doing. I pick her up and wipe away some of the dirt covering her.

"You look like a sad doll. Why are you by yourself, and how long have you been here? I'm going to take you to the bigger room so I can check you out in the light coming in from the doorway."

I pick up my flashlight and shine it past her and down the tunnel. I wonder how far it goes. It's hard to see with this crappy light.

"Let's go, sad doll. I'll take care of you. But I can't bring you into

49

Momma Johnson's house because then she'll find out about my secret hiding place, and I can't let that happen. You see, I'm a foster kid, and, just like you, people kinda leave me places and forget about me. And I need a place to hide in case I ever need to get away. Momma Johnson seems like a great lady, but other ladies have seemed nice, and it turns out they're not. So, I can't risk her finding this place in case I need it."

We reach the room, and I hold her in the light.

"Boy, you're pretty old…" I sniff her. "Man, do you stink! But don't worry. I'll wash your clothes for you. That'll help you feel better."

I take her clothes off really carefully because it seems like her arms and legs are barely attached with only some thread and a few buttons. When her shirt is off, I see the name Patty stitched onto her chest, right over where her heart would be if she were a real person. I trace the letters.

"Some girl must have really loved you because she sewed her mark into you. I bet you got lost down here because if she loved you that much, Patty wouldn't leave you here on purpose." I wipe some more dirt off her face.

I wonder who Patty is and why she left her doll here—

I swing the flashlight back toward the tunnel. Did Patty get lost in there?

Patty. Who are you, and why were you in this dark and scary tunnel? Were you trying to hide from people hurting you? That's why I like to find the perfect hiding places. This way, when someone hurts me, I can hide somewhere. What happened to you? I know that you wouldn't leave your baby doll down here on purpose.

Did you get lost in there? My goosebumps come back at the thought. I clear my throat and shake my head to stop thinking about just how scary it is, and instead, I look back at the doll. "Okay, I'm going to call you Patty after your owner. How does that sound?" Patty's stinky smell doesn't stop me from hugging her. "Nice to meet you, Patt—"

"Anna?"

Uh oh. That sounds like Ms. Nellie Inez. I have to get out of here before she sees me and tells Momma Jay.

I prop Patty against the dirt wall. "I promise I'll be back soon with clean clothes," I whisper. "And I won't forget you. I'll take you home with me and give you a place to live. That's what people do for me since I don't have a mom like you. But I promise I won't hurt you like people have me. I'll take care of you. I don't like being alone, so I won't ever do that to you. Bye, Patty."

With the flashlight and her dirty clothes tucked in my shirt, I scale the ladder while holding my apple for Rose. Right as I'm about to take the last step. The sound of snapping sticks in the forest warns me of someone standing outside the opening.

That's *not* good.

Chapter 6
Cornrows

"Greetings, feathered friends. You sound so beautiful today." Ms. Nellie Inez speaks to the birds as if they can understand her.

The cracking sound of twigs gets closer. I'm frozen, gripping the old metal ladder tightly. If I move, Ms. Nellie Inez will hear it rattling. *Just hold still, Anna. Don't move.*

I try to ignore the darkness. Right now, everything looks incredibly creepy. I squeeze my eyes closed and quickly turn back toward the ladder.

"Well, well, well, look here. How in the heck did the door to the slave tunnel get opened?" She groans as she lifts the door off the ground.

"Ugh. You're heavy, and I don't understand why you're open, but let's close you to prevent animals from getting hurt." She's talking to the door.

What the heck am I gonna do? If I holler, my hiding place is gone forever.

The door slams with such force that I can swear it might cause an earthquake. And now, I'm stuck.

The ladder sways back and forth with me on it. My heart feels like it's going to beat through my chest. *Please don't break. Please.* My knuckles throb, and my palms sweat, but there's nothing I can do about it right now. Letting go of this ladder isn't an option. It's too dark for me to climb back down. What if it breaks when I move? Nope, staying right where I am is the best choice.

There could be a creature at the bottom of the ladder, waiting for me to fall so it could eat me. Or worse, there could be mummies coming to life now that it's dark. Or vampires getting ready to suck all my blood out.

Stop it. This is not helping. I squeeze the ladder tightly and hold my breath. I'll be trapped forever if I knock this ladder off the wall.

I slowly let out all the air I'm holding in my lungs and get ready for what's about to happen.

Finally, the ladder stops. I'm terrified right now as I turn my head to look around. This damn place is scary when the flashlight is off. *Sorry, Daddy. I know I promised not to swear, but right now is a good time to do it.*

There's complete darkness. The musty scent of the dusty room seems to take over everything. The smells fill my nose, my mouth, and my eyes. I can't hear anything, making it difficult to determine if Ms. Nellie Inez is above me.

And then I feel a sneeze coming on.

I take another breath and hold it to stop the sneeze.

"Ah-choo!"

That didn't work.

But Ms. Nellie Inez must not still be up there. I need to try to get out of here.

I reach over my head to the door and push.

Nothing happens.

I try again. It's super heavy and doesn't budge. My arms shake from the weight. I lift it an inch or so, and for a second, I see some light. But it's too heavy; it slams back down, and the light disappears.

What if I can't open this? What if I'm stuck in here, and no one knows? I could die in my new hiding place. I could die down here.

I'm Anna, and I'm strong. There's no way I'll die like this. With all my strength, I press my back against the door, and push as hard as I can. *Come on, Anna, don't stop. You got this.*

53

Finally, my head is above the ground, but the weight of the door hurts my neck. I keep pushing, going up another rung, and then the door flings open. Seeing the sky has never made me so happy before. I duck down fast, hoping Ms. Nellie Inez isn't standing around somewhere.

Then I hear a branch crack. Snap. *What was that?* I look around and see a baby deer. "Well, hello, baby. Where's your momma?"

The tiny deer sticks her head up and stares at me.

"You should not be out here alone. A bear could eat you. Or even a coyote. You know what? Just like you, I don't want to be out here by myself either."

The small deer keeps her eyes on me, but she doesn't look afraid. Maybe she could be my friend.

I stand on the ground, then say into the hole, "Bye, Patty. I'll come see you tomorrow and bring back some clean clothes for you."

Carefully, I lower the heavy door back to the ground. *Phew.* I'm thankful I got out of that one. I'll have to locate some batteries for this flashlight so I can use it tomorrow.

As I turn to leave, the momma deer pops her head out from behind a tree.

"Are you here to grab your baby? She sure is pretty." I blow the tiny deer a kiss. "If you're here tomorrow, I'm certain I'll lay eyes on you. Maybe I should give you a name. We all have names. How about Spot? Yup, that will work. Bye, Spot. Maybe I'll see you tomorrow."

***

"How's y'all peanut butter po'boy?"

I lick the strawberry jelly off my bottom lip. "It was super good, thank you." I smile at Momma Johnson, who sits with me at the table where she's eating something that has nasty onions and peppers in it.

"*Chère*, we hafta talk 'bout de school, *demain*."

All of a sudden, my sandwich doesn't taste so good.

"Momma Johnson, what is *demain*?" I might as well get used to asking her questions every time I don't know what she's talking about.

"Ah, *demain* de mean ah… on the morrow?" She smiles.

Does she think I should understand her now?

"On the morrow? Next ah day. Tom…" She rubs her chin.

"Tomorrow?" I ask.

54

"*Oui.*" She nods.

"Would ya like a mey to makes y'all hair?" She points at my head. "Aah make dat look bedder if y'all like." She tugs one of her braids.

I shrug. "Why not? Sure."

Momma Jay, as usual, claps her hands when she's happy.

"Afta y'all eat, aah draw y'all bathroom water."

"Bathroom water?"

I feel like a piece of my sandwich is stuck in my throat. I gag.

Momma Jay jumps up from her chair and hits me on my back. But I wasn't choking; it'd just gotten stuck for a second. "Um, Momma Johnson? Did you... uh... say... a *bath*?" I look at my lap and dig my nails into my palm.

"*Chère*, can ya look at a mey?" Her voice soft.

My sandwich feels as heavy as a brick, and I drop what's left onto my plate.

Momma Jay touches my hand. "*Chère*, does y'all not like a bath?"

Right now, all I can do is shake my head. I'm afraid I'll vomit my entire sandwich onto the table if I even budge. Momma Jay sits and watches me without saying anything. "I enjoy taking showers. That's the only thing we had in my last foster home with Mrs. Dorsey," I whisper. *Please don't make me take a bath.*

Momma Jay moves closer. "Well, den, shower it's gonna be. Does y'all knows how t'work de shower?"

I squeak back, "Yes. I do."

"Wonderful. After de shower, we does y'all hair to make pretty." She picks up my plate. "Does y'all wanna anoder po'boy?" I've never had as much food to eat as I do in this foster home. I went to bed hungry all the time with Mother and Mrs. Dorsey, so I knew they didn't love me because they didn't care if I was hungry or not. Momma Jay always asks me if I'd like something to eat. I wonder if this means that she loves me.

"No, I'm good. I'll go take a shower. But thank you for asking." I'm not used to anyone

asking me what I want. It will take some getting used to.

Momma Johnson cocks her head. "*Chère*, can aah talk with y'all?"

I twist my fingers together at her too-serious tone and nod.

My heart beats fast and loud, like drums. This is how I know that something is bothering me.

"Did y'all gets hurt in de bathroom in de other foster places?"

55

How did she find out? Did Mrs. Alex find out from Mother and call Momma Johnson to tell her about it? Great. Just *great*. Now she probably thinks I'm dirty, just like Derek said people would when he hurt me.

I am *not* going to let her think I'm dirty. "No one has hurt me in the bathroom."

She squeezes my hand. "Well, if y'all feel a much bedder, y'all can a lock de door to de room of bath. Aah fixin' dat makin' ya feel bedder."

I look up, and she winks. "Now, let's get ya showered so we can do y'all hair for *demain*." She hits the table, then rises to her feet. "Mais, *chère*, meet mey in de room of de living and we can watch de funny guys whiles aah makes pretty hair." She giggles.

Right when I believe I can make sense of her words, she adds to my confusion. "Did you say you wanted me to meet you in the living room to do my hair for tomorrow?"

She grabs a dishcloth and then turns toward me.

"*Oui, ma belle.*"

"What does *oui* and the other thing you said, ma… ma… bell… something mean?"

Momma Johnson giggles some more, but she's not hurting my feelings because it's not mean laughter. "Well, Boo, in my language, *oui* means *yes*. And *ma belle* means *my pretty girl*."

She thinks I'm pretty. *Wow*. No one has ever called me pretty before.

I like it.

I head to the bathroom.

But I still listen at the door once I close it just to make sure.

Momma Jay is singing in the kitchen as she cleans up. That's all I can hear.

Great, I can finally take a shower without any worries. I glance around the wooden bathroom made of logs. *This place is so much nicer than Mrs. Dorsey's.*

As I remove the old doll clothes from my sweater, an apple slips out.

Oh, darn. I forgot to give this to Rose. I guess that just means I'll have to take it to her tomorrow. Yay—another visit with the horse!

I jump in the shower with the doll clothes, then wash them with Momma Jay's shampoo. Once I'm back in my bedroom and all done with the shower, I tuck the clean doll clothes under my pillow next to my doll.

"Hey, Raggedy, I met someone today you may like. I'll bring her home soon so you won't feel lonely anymore and have someone just like you. I know you're sad because I know what it feels like to be alone."

"*Chère*, y'all comin'?" Momma Jay calls from the living room.

Heading out to join her, I grab my brother's bear, Teddy, from the bed.

Momma Jay points to a spot in front of her with a brush in her hand. "Sit, *chère*. Aah make your hair *belle*."

"What does that mean?" I ask.

She shakes her head. "It a means a be… aut…

I can tell she's struggling, so I finish the word for her. "Beautiful?"

She claps. "Ahh, yes, *chère*. That de word."

She points to the pillow and, at the same time, laughs at the men on the television show. "They's make funny." She giggles more.

Once I sit down on the yellow pillow she has on the floor, Momma Jay settles her legs around me. She brushes my hair, and the soft bristles tickle my scalp. We watch one episode, then another, then another. Before long, two hours had passed.

"Aah done." She holds up the mirror so I can see what she did to my hair.

"Whoa." I run my hands over a bunch of tiny braids all over my head. She even put beads in them—orange, purple, and green. They look like the colors of autumn.

Momma Johnson whispers in my ear, "Does y'all like it?"

"I do like it. It looks cool." My bum is numb from sitting on the small pillow for so long, but I totally lost track of time because Momma Jay had been talking to me the whole time. Getting the braids did hurt a little, but since I knew she was just trying to make my hair look better, I didn't complain. Maybe this new hairdo will stop the kids from making fun of me tomorrow on my first day.

Looking at myself in the mirror now, I'm glad she did this. I do look pretty.

Momma Jay taps my shoulder. "Who did y'all hair before this." She points to my head.

"One of my foster sisters didn't like me much when I first started living with Mrs. Dorsey. She cut all my long curls off one night when I was sleeping."

Momma Jay gasps and puts her hand over her mouth. "Dat's a mean girl."

"At first, she was, but we became friends the longer I lived with her. She tried to fix it after she cut it, but it didn't work. That's why I had long pieces of hair and short ones all over the place."

At the mention of my wolf pack sisters, my heart hurts. I was just with them a few days ago. I bet they're all hanging out in the bedroom together right now. I wish we were still together, but not at Mrs. Dorsey's.

It would've been groovy cool if they could've moved with me here. They would like Momma Jay because I do.

"*Chère*, does y'all wants t'talk 'bout Mrs. Dorsey?"

One of my other foster moms, Jessica, and her husband used to ask me questions all the time when I lived with them before Mrs. Dorsey. Jessica always wanted to talk about my feelings about this and that… But what good did it do me? They still made me leave, and they let Mrs. Alex take my brother from me. So, what good are feelings? No one cares. If they did, my brother would be sitting on this floor next to me instead of me holding his bear on my lap—the stuffed bear he dropped when they ripped him out of my arms.

"No, I don't want to talk about Mrs. Dorsey. It just makes me mad to do so."

"S'okay. Does cornrows make you happy?" She looks concerned as we both stand to go to bed, and she has her hand on my back.

A lot of being here with her is making me happy. Being happy makes me nervous because any time I've been happy before, something ruins it. But I can't hurt her feelings since she's being so nice. And I do want to be happy. "Yes, I'm happy, and I like them. Thanks, Momma Jay."

"Mais, *chère, il fait gris*?"

I look at her.

"Ahh. Dat means it's, ah, a… long day. Fixin' go make doe-doe."

I try to talk in the middle of chuckling. "Yes, it's been a long day for me, too, and I'm ready to go to sleep. Or, should I say, make doe-doe?" As we make our way through the kitchen, we laugh together.

"*Chère*"

"Yes?"

'Does y'all wants mey to tuck y'all into de bed?"

"What?" With just that one question, I feel my legs turn into cement.

Chapter 7
Stars

"Thank you, Momma Jay. I can put myself to bed and tuck myself in."

Before speaking again, she glances at the ground and then looks up. "How 'bout I come in later and turn de lights off before ya makes doe-doe?" She cocks her head.

Maybe this would be okay. She's done nothing that makes me think she wants girl time or anything like Sue did.

"Why not." Slowly, I nod, then head into the bathroom to brush my teeth and wash my face. When I'm done, I kneel by my bed.

Hello, Jesus. I'm still here, living with Momma Jay. Tomorrow is my first day at a new school. You and I both know that school is not my thing. Kids are mean. But I guess some are nice.

I take a deep breath and push my hands together harder. *I can't believe the difference in my hair after Momma Jay braided it and added beads. She's friendly so far, and I think she likes me. Please let her stay that way. She did tell me she would take me to your house this coming Sunday. I have six days to go since it's only Monday.*

I open my eyes and take in the view of my pretty room that smells like the forest. As I look around, the stars shining through my bedroom window capture my attention. I cross my legs as I sit on the wooden floor in front of the window; I love looking at the sky—especially because I can usually find the big and little dippers. The stars don't change. When I look at them, I realize that my world is the same; it's just the people and locations that keep changing. I feel better. And not like a strange alien moving from one planet to another.

I stare at the stars for a bit, then yawn. *Well, I hope you sleep good, or, as Momma Jay would say, make good doe-doe, Jesus. I'll chat with you tomorrow. I'm getting tired and going to sleep now."*

I look at the woods where I'd stumbled upon my newest hiding place. *Goodnight, Patty. I'll see you tomorrow.* I blow a kiss into the air, hoping it reaches her.

As I settle into my cozy bed with my blankets, Raggedy, and Teddy, Momma Jay knocks on the door.

"Come in."

The door cracks open, and only her head appears, with, as always, her cheerful face. "Make good doe-doe."

"Goodnight to you, too, Momma Jay,"

"Y'all feel good in de bed? De blankets are warm for ya?"

I can tell she wants to make sure that I'm okay by all her questions.

"Do you want to come in?" I ask.

"Only if y'all 'k wid dat." Even across the room, I see the big smile spread across her face. She walks to sit on the chest at the end of my bed.

"Dis is mey favorite room in de house. I thought ya woulda like it. So, I moved mey room to de spare room so y'all can have dis one."

"You did that for me?" I can't believe it. She moved out of here so I could have this beautiful one. No one has ever done something like that for me before. No one. Not even Daddy.

"Sure did, *chère*. She smooths out the blankets at the end of the bed with her hands. "Y'all needs a nice room. Now make good doe-doe, and I see y'all in de morning." Momma Jay walks to the door and switches off the light.

"Aah happy y'all here wid a mey."

She pulls the door shut behind her.

I find myself alone in my dimly lit room for another night. The faint light on my back deck pierces the darkness, reminding me of my earlier feeling of being trapped. I'll never feel stuck there again because it's my special place to hide. In the past, I've been in situations where I felt trapped and couldn't do anything, like the times when I had to leave my first daddy and my brother Curtis.

A sniffle slips out. "Daddy, I miss you so much," I whisper.

Tears trickle down both cheeks, and I bury my face in Raggedy.

I tried to hold onto you, Curtis. When Mrs. Alex took you from me. I'm sorry I wasn't strong enough.

Multiple times throughout the night, I jolt awake and look at the door, waiting for someone to enter—I'll never sleep comfortably again after Derek. And no one else since him has really given me a reason to. I completely forgot to put the chair in front of the door.

Do I really need it?

Momma Jay knocks and asks to come in, before she enters my room. She's never just walked in.

Nah., I don't think I need to move the chair tonight.

Go back to sleep, Anna. No one will come through the door and Momma Jay is sleeping. I tell myself this over and over until I...

***

"Let's all greet Anna Snow as she joins our classroom today." The teacher, Mrs. Song, introduces me to all the kids.

Momma Jay dropped me off this morning so I wouldn't have to sit on the bus with the mean girls. Well, she hadn't phrased it that way, but that was what she meant when she'd said it while we were having grits for breakfast.

Mrs. Song has me stand in front of the classroom like I've had to do at each new school I've gone to. I hate doing this; it makes me feel like a brand-new toy at a toy store—and an ugly one at that because kids usually point and burst into laughter.

"Find your seat and hold your smirking," she says to a few of them.

A girl with red hair raises her hand.

"Yes, Cassie, what do you need?" asks Mrs. Song.

Cassie moves her long, red hair to over her shoulder with a flick. "Mrs. Song, why does her hair look so funny?"

Yup, the class laughs. Just like always.

"Cassie, if you can't say any kind words, don't say anything at all." The teacher shakes her head at the girl.

This doesn't stop that girl, though. "And why does she have one eyebrow and big teeth?"

More laughter—this time, pretty much everybody does it. It's going to be another bad time at this school.

Mrs. Song gives her a stern look and raises her voice. "Young lady, make your way to the office immediately."

Cassie doesn't budge. If she hadn't been mean to me, I might have been impressed with her not being scared of a teacher.

I always try to stay on the teacher's good side. But I guess Cassie doesn't have to if no one's laughing at her.

Mrs. Song walks past me, and she leans into Cassie, their faces really close. "Move it immediately."

Now it's Mrs. Song's turn to not budge.

With a loud *crack*, Cassie shoves her chair into her desk after she finally stands up. Then she stomps away and slams the classroom door.

Wow. I can't imagine doing that in a teacher's room. I always try to *not* get in trouble.

Once again, Mrs. Song stands beside me at the front of the classroom, and I realize who Cassie is. Momma Jay had said the neighbor girl who owns the black horse is named Cassie. She also told me that Cassie would be in my class, as there is only one 4th grader in this school.

Well, I guess that was her. And she's not going to like me now, for sure.

Darn, I'd wanted to visit her horse, but she's not going to let me now. Not after I got her sent to the office. Of course, I might be able to visit him in secret, maybe right before it gets dark.

As I continue to stand in front of the class with the teacher standing next to me again, another girl, raises her hand.

"Yes, Michelle?" the teacher asks.

"I like her hair. I wish my mother would do that to mine." She smiles at me.

"Thank you, Michelle, for being kind." Mrs. Song looks down at me, then at Michelle, and back at me again. Teachers have a tendency to do this when they want you to answer a question or say something. That's not going to happen. I take in a deep breath instead.

Oh no! The room starts to get fuzzy. *Not now, Anna. Not now. You cannot pass out here.* My heart pounds against my chest, and my hands start to sweat. This is what happens before I fall and can't remember anything. I have to think of something else. How much longer will she keep me standing here facing everyone like a circus act?

"Take your seats, please. We need to get today started." Mrs. Song walks to her desk and pulls out a black book.

"Rebecca?"

"Here."

"Steven?"

"Here."

I'll never remember all these names. Why should I? I won't be here long before Mrs. Alex moves me again.

"Con…"

The classroom door slams shut like a firecracker as Cassie walks back into the classroom. She stops in front of me after she hands Mrs. Song a note. I really want to punch this girl in the face. She acts like she is better than me. Well… Maybe she is. I'm sure she has a nice family and lives in a nice house. I'm sure her mommy and daddy both want her.

Maybe she is better than me. But I still want to punch her.

Thinking about punching Cassie makes my heart slow down, and my hands are in fists now rather than sweating.

"The principal told me to come back to class. That was a fun trip." With a flick of her hair, she returns to her seat.

Mrs. Song clears her throat. "Ms. Anna Snow recently relocated to the Inez ranch and is now living with Ms. Maude Johnson."

"Moved in? She moved into the black lady's house?" Cassie snickers. "Who wants to live on Ms. Nellie Inez's property? Eww. She's a poor, old lady." Cassie wrinkles her nose as she laughs at me.

"Um, Mrs. Song, what do you mean she just moved in? Where are her parents?" Michelle watches me as she asks the question. I feel like unwanted trash—unloved and abandoned—just standing here.

"She's a foster child who recently relocated to our school and settled with a new family. Not all of us can live with our moms and dads."

In a single moment, she completely tears me apart with her words in front of everyone. I clench my fists tightly, and my nails seem to be turning into pins that dig deeper into my hands. All the students are staring at me as if I'm a freak. Yup, that's right; I'm the main attraction in *this* classroom's new strange and bizarre show.

Everywhere, hands shoot up in the air. A boy in the third row catches her attention.

"Yes, Ben?" Mrs. Song gestures toward him with one hand while her other rests on my shoulder.

"What's a foster child?" He stutters, and his voice sounds just like a frog's.

I dig my fingernails harder into my skin. If only I could give this teacher a swift kick in the leg right now. How can she possibly be this dumb to make me stand up here for this? I'm sure she wouldn't want to showcase all *her* bad stuff to the rest of the teachers in the school. I imagine her standing before a crowd in the auditorium, sharing all about her business.

Cassie is the next person to raise her hand, which isn't a surprise. And I'm sure what she's going to say is going to be mean.

"That old black bitch takes in kids no one wants and whose parents don't want them anymore. I guess nobody wants good ol' Anna Snow." She says it loud enough that everyone has to hear it—and she looks mighty pleased with herself for doing so.

"Cassie, no more talking." Mrs. Song smacks a hand onto Cassie's desk. "Keep your mouth closed."

I march right over to Cassie's desk and shove her books so they go flying across the classroom. "Are you asking for a broken nose? If you dare to call my new foster mother an old black bitch one more time, I'll make sure your teeth end up like your nose—broken."

I snap out of my daydream about sticking up to Cassie when Mrs. Song says, "Take a seat, Anna." She points her finger toward the empty seat next to the window.

"Class, pull out your math books, as today we are working on math problems," she announces.

Great. The window is by my desk so I can look outside when I get bored. Math is not my thing, and I will definitely get bored in this class.

Soon enough, the school bell signals the start of recess. Before I can even push in my chair, Michelle stops at my desk while kids run by her to get outside.

"Anna, would you like to play with me for recess?" Michelle looks poor and that's how I looked when I lived with Mrs. Dorsey. Her hair looks like it's wet but it's not, and she's wearing dirty clothes with holes in her sneakers. Is she a foster child, too? I'll have to ask her at recess.

"Move out of the way, scum," Cassie says, shoving Michelle aside.

"That girl is mean. Stay away from her, Anna. Do you want to jump?" She stands waiting for me to answer.

"No thanks." I slowly shove my chair into my desk.

"Okay. If you change your mind, you can join me." Michelle runs ahead of me once we're outside. She heads toward the ropes.

Everyone else pairs up and starts playing together while I'm left standing there. I decide to play with some small rocks at my feet and think about when I'd skip rocks with Curtis.

"Come with me, Anna Snow," calls Michelle from across the playground. "Let's jump rope!" She grabs my hand and pulls me toward the other girls who are already swinging the ropes.

"Anna Snow's gonna jump with us." Michelle is surprisingly loud for how small she is. I'm a lot taller than her, so I have to look down at her when we talk.

"Michelle, you can call me Anna."

"Okay, Anna. Let's jump."

"I bet she sucks," Cassie yells from behind me.

"Shut up, Cassie!" Michelle screams at her.

"Let's go, Anna." Michelle claps her hands together as the ropes start spinning.

I stand watching, not wanting to do anything right now. Cassie stands behind me with a bunch of her friends. I hate people watching me and, worse, picking on me.

"Come on, Anna! Hop in!" The girls twirling the ropes holler.

"I bet she's no good, and that's why she's acting like a scaredy cat." Cassie's words burn my ears. No one calls me a scaredy cat. I mean, no one.

I do as instructed and, before long, I'm in one of my happy places, with ropes circling me as I jump to their rhythm. The ropes go faster, and I follow. The beads in my braids hit my forehead as I bounce over one rope and then the next. I'm not good at a lot of things, but I feel good about myself as I jump ropes because this is not something that a lot of girls can do. I may be a foster kid that no one wants, but girls want me to jump rope with them. When I'm jumping, all the bad things go away.

"Cassie, you're not nearly as good at this as she is," Michelle says.

More people are gathering around where I'm jumping. My legs appear to be moving on their own faster and faster.

"I want to jump now. It's my turn." A girl that I've never met tells the twirlers.

Though the ropes stop spinning, my legs, for a brief second, still feel like they're moving. Then—they begin to throb.

65

Thank goodness that girl wanted a turn and they stopped because I would not quit. I never quit the awful book games with Derek where he would stack books on my and Curtis' arms 'til we dropped them. I'd refused to quit then for Derek, and I refuse to quit today for Cassie. But this is tough and I'm sweaty. I use my sleeve to wipe the sweat from my forehead.

"Who punched you in the face?" Cassie shouts. "Look, everyone! She has a bruise on her cheek."

I can no longer hold back. I step out of the ropes to stand nose-to-nose in front of Cassie. "If you say another mean thing to me, *you* will be the one to have a bruise on her face." I lean in and lock eyes with her. "Now, *back off.*"

Cassie doesn't move for a second, but then she flicks her long hair, and it almost hits me in the face.

"*Whatever*, girl nobody wants." She walks away quickly with her friends.

Good thing because, I swear, I would've punched her for sure.

When we return to class, we finish the day with spelling words. Minus Cassie, the first day was just okay. My hairstyle was a hit with many kids, and some were curious enough to want to touch it. That was kinda cool.

***

Momma Jay is waiting outside when I leave the school. Cassie walks behind me.

"Look, everyone, the foster kid is leaving. The kid no one wants except for an old black bitch. No white people would want her."

I can see Momma Jay glaring from the car, so I wonder if she can hear Cassie. Momma Jay doesn't usually have a mean look on her face.

Cassie and her friends walk next to me as I get closer to Momma Jay's car to leave school. "There's your old black bitch to pick you up. Go home now foster kid." I close the car door. The window is down, so I know Momma Jay heard her.

"Dat is the mean Cassie girl. See why I don't want ya t'go visit de black horse. Stay aways from dat mean girl." Her eyebrows are pushed together, making her look mad.

"I will. I don't like her much. She's been in my face all day and saying mean things about me."

"Member dis. *Chère.* If someone makin' fun of ya. It's a dem dat is jealous of ya." She turns quickly and winks at me. "I betcha she's jealous of ya cool lookin' braids."

"I bet you're right, Momma Jay." I smile back at her, though I'm faking it.

There's no way Cassie is jealous of me. Why would she be? I have nothing, and no one wants me. Nope, Cassie is not jealous. She wants to hurt me.

As soon as I get into the house, the smell of something yummy fills my nose.

Momma Jay dances from the front door to the kitchen. Food covers the entire table. There's not one inch that is open.

"I say we… we… mmm… make a party."

"Oh. That sounds fun." But really it doesn't. Today was hard and that's always the case for me when I'm around kids. I hate being reminded that I'm a reject. But Momma Jay seems happy as she dances back to the kitchen and puts my books on the counter top.

I try hard to act happy when I walk to the kitchen table because I know she worked hard on this food all day, and I don't want to make her feel sad.

Then, out of nowhere, Momma Jay grabs me and pulls me into a tight hug.

"Aah knows ya told mey ya don't like peoples touching ya, but ya looks like ya just needin' someone to love ya."

I wasn't expecting that, so I just stood still with my hands down along my legs. She's absolutely right. I don't like people touching me, and the tighter she squeezes, the more frozen I am. What else is she going to do to me?

Maybe I should push her away and run. But where? And what would I say to her?

Thankfully, she lets me go then.

"Well, aah glad y'all home. Aah fixin' a fias doe-doe for us tonight." She claps.

"Um, what?" I grin at her.

Momma Jay turns up some music I've never heard before. I'm surprised that it helps me feel better and makes me want to dance. "Well, *chère*, we fixin' de dance party wida lot a food. We's gotta some jambalaya, wida some a coconut mango sticky rice and some bread puddin'." She licks her lips. "Aah dink y'all shoulda like a de puddin' and de sticky rice. If y'all don't like de jambalaya, y'all don't gotta eat it." Her hands wave in the air to the beat of the music. Then she turns away from me, and all I can see are her hips moving as she shuffles across the kitchen floor.

I can't stop myself from staring at her as she dances back to the stove because this lady isn't like anyone I've known before. She's funny and seems really nice. Are most people like her, and I just got bad foster parents?

Momma Jay holds out her hand, covered with an oven mitt. "Dance wida mey."

She doesn't give me a chance to respond before she twirls me around in a circle under her arm. Before long, I'm doing the dance that I used to do at Daddy's house when he would play with the band in the garage. I'm laughing so hard, I'm louder than the music—and that means I'm *really* loud. But Momma Jay doesn't seem to mind. Unlike Mother used to.

This is really nice—not getting yelled at while I'm having fun.

After what seems like an hour, we sit at the table to eat, with legs tired from dancing. Momma Jay picks up the plate and is all set to put a scoop of jam… bal… lula. on it, but I stop her. "Um, Momma Jay? Do I have to eat that?"

She freezes while holding the spoon in mid-air. "Mais, s'okay, *chère*." Her face does not look mad at me. Maybe that means that everything's all right and she's not upset, but she continues to stay locked on my face. "I don't like vegetables and other stuff in the soup. Could I try some other things instead?"

Instantly, Momma Jay moves the spoon and points it at another dish. "Ya can eats what ya likes, no problem. Does ya want t'try dis?" She holds the spoon over the bread pudding.

"Okay, I'll try that instead. I mean, mmm, bread and pudding mixed together; it has to be yummy. I like both of those things."

I can't help but feel good as Momma Jay puts the plate in front of me—she actually cares about what I want. In the time that I've lived here with her, she has shown me so much love—

Could she love me? Daddy did in my first foster home, even though I'd had to leave because he hadn't been able to keep me safe from Derek. Jessica and her husband had acted as if they really cared, too, but… *did* they? They'd let Mrs. Alex take my *brother* away from me.

All I can say for sure right now is that Momma Jay acts like she cares. She always wants to know what I want to do for fun. She asks me what I want to eat. And she always knocks on my bedroom door before she comes in. These are things people do when they care about you.

I take a bite of the bread pudding. It's incredible. The bread melts in my mouth like candy but tastes like cinnamon with a little ice cream flavor. But there's not any ice cream on it. "Mmmm. This is fantastic!"

"Aah glad y'all likes it, *chère*. Now, tell me 'bout de good dings dat happened in de school today?" She taps my hand.

"It was okay. I made a new friend named Michelle. She likes to jump rope like I do. She said she really likes my hair and whishes someone would do that to hers." I take a bite of the coconut sticky rice mixed with mango. "Whoa. This is so good, too!"

"Aah glad you like mey food." Her eyes sparkle as if she's just won a prize.

"Momma Jay, after I eat, can I take an apple to Rose?"

"Yes. When ya done eatin' ya can fetch a apple from de fridge."

I'm so glad she answers my questions quickly, not like some of the other foster parents who might not even bother answering.

I take the last bite of my bread pudding, then stand up with my plate.

"I got dis. Aah fixin' t'clean, so no need for ya t'help. Go fun outdoors." She takes the plate out of my hand.

"Momma Jay, how do I say thanks in your language?"

Her face lights up. "*Merci beaucoup.* Lemme say dat again slowly for y'all. *Mer... ci... Beau... coup.*"

"*Merci beaucoup.* Momma Jay." My body feels warm all over.

"Y'all welcome, *chère.*" She bows at me like she's on stage.

"Nows have fun. But be back by dark." She spins away from the table, takes the dishes to the sink, and heads down the hallway toward the bathroom.

I can't wait to see Patty. I jump up from the table quickly so I can get outside. *Wait.* I need batteries for that darn flashlight. Quietly, I open one drawer, then another, and another 'til I find them. There's no way I can ask Momma Jay if I can use them because she'll ask me why, and I can't tell her about my hiding place. I feel bad taking them without asking first, but I have to right now if I want to help Patty.

Chapter 8
Patty

I grab Patty's clean clothes, the flashlight, a pink ribbon for her hair, and a small brush.

I pull my hooded sweatshirt over my clothes, making sure I have everything in the pocket, then walk through my bedroom door just as Momma Jay calls my name. I quickly dash to my bed and tuck the flashlight under my brother's bear.

Momma Jay knocks on my door. "*Chère?* Here's de apple for de horse."

Crap. I got so busy looking for batteries that I forgot about the apple.

I move fast to get the door for her. "I almost forgot."

She hands me the apple. "I do dat all de time—forget dings. Be back soon--Aah don't wantcha in de woods in de dark."

"I will."

"Have a fun." She shuts my door behind her. I really like that. She doesn't keep my door open and still knocks before she comes in.

I tuck the flashlight and apple in my sweater, then head off on my adventure.

Hello Forest. I'm going to run through you again, so don't make all kinds of creepy noises.

I notice a big stick lying on the ground. *This is perfect.* I pick it up and swing it in the air. Maybe this will scare an animal away if I need it.

Here we go. I walk slowly at first, telling myself not to be scared. Then, a loud cracking noise changes things for me, and I throw down my stick and run fast.

Phew. I bend over to catch my breath on the other side of the forest path.

"Hello, Rose, I didn't forget you this time." I sit on the top railing, watching the horse prance around the pasture.

She heads toward me slowly, but she's definitely interested in me.

"You smell the treat, huh?"

Her lips brush my palm as she takes the apple.

"I bet apples for you are like ice cream for me."

She allows me to pet her long nose for a second before she turns and runs along the fence line. I wonder if she doesn't like me. Thunder would never leave my side. I bend down and begin to crawl under the fence when I hear someone clear their throat.

'What are you doing?"

I look up and see Ms. Nellie Inez standing there.

"I… um… was going inside to visit Rose?" I look down and play with the grass.

"That is not a good idea. You could get hurt in there if Rose got rambunctious."

Slowly, I move back to the other side of the fence and stand up next to Ms. Nellie Inez. "I'm sorry, but I just wanted to get closer to Rose. She doesn't let me pet her long."

"Yeah, you are right about that. She is moody. Sometimes, she likes you to pet her, and other times, she just wants you to admire her." Ms. Nellie Inez whistled. In seconds, Rose comes trotting over to both of us.

"Whoa! How'd you do that?" I try to whistle.

Ms. Nellie Inez laughs. "I think you may need to practice that one." She whistles again.

Rose moves her head right against Ms. Nellie Inez's face and lets her rub her.

"How's it going with Mrs. Johnson?"

"Good." Rose moves in my direction, and I begin to pet her nose. "I like her. She's nice to me."

"That doesn't surprise me. She's a nice lady. Well, Rose, I have to make my rounds on the farm." Ms. Nellie Inez tips her hat to Rose and me.

"No going under that fence. You could get hurt. Got it." Her voice is stern.

"Got it. I'll stay on the outside." I smile, hoping it will help her to believe me.

"Another thing, be careful walking around the woods. I saw an old hatch door that opens to a deep hole. Make sure you are not walking around in the dark. You'd break both your legs if you fell in that old thing.

"Okay, I will. Momma Jay wants me home before dark anyway."

"Momma Jay?" She tilts her head to the side. "I like it. Okay, kid, I'm sure I'll see you

around out here sometime.

"Bye. And thank you for letting me visit your horse."

Ms. Nellie Inez walks away from me, waving her hand in the air.

I don't hear her crunching the tree branches anymore. I don't think Ms. Nellie Inez would like me playing in her dark hole. But I always need a place to hide, and that is a perfect spot.

It's time to go get Patty out of that dark place. "Bye, Rose. You probably can't hear me, but I'll come visit you again tomorrow."

I shake my head as I get close to the forest tree line. Here I go again. But I'm going to make myself walk slowly. When I run, I get more scared. I got this.

Just as I enter the forest, I hear the sound of a bird squawk. I jump. *Anna, it's a bird. Let's think of all the cool animals that live in a forest.* I like to give my mind some other things to think about when I'm scared. There's a deer, worms, snakes, birds, rabbits and…

Just as I reach the secret door, I slow down. Someone or something is walking behind me. I stop; it stops. I walk; it walks. *Anna, don't turn around. This is just your mind trying to scare you.*

By the time I manage to open the secret door, whatever it is will have enough time to eat me. Running back to Rose is impossible because something stands between us. I could run home, but then Patty would have to spend another night alone in the darkness.

Slowly, I turn. Then I see it—the baby deer is following me! This baby must like me. This is the second time she's been around me. I'm so happy; I can't wait to make her my friend. But I have to talk calmly so I don't scare her away.

"Spot. Hi, how are you doing? Did you miss me?" I walk toward her to see if she'll let me get close. I take one step, then another. Before long, I'm in front of her. I extend my arm and leave it there. Within a few seconds, she comes closer and allows me to touch her nose.

"Well, thank you for letting me pet you. You are so pretty, and I've never had a pet deer before." I glance around to see her mom—she should be nearby. "I'd love to hang with you and play, but I don't want to make your mommy mad at me. I reach out to pet her nose some more. Spot does not turn away.

"Are you used to humans? Why aren't you afraid of me? You don't know me? Can you tell that I won't hurt you because I'm moving slowly so I don't scare you?" Spot moves her head to the side like she's looking for something in the woods, but she doesn't move away from me. I stop trying to pet her because I don't want her to think that she can't leave if she doesn't want to.

Spot turns and looks at me and steps backward. "It was nice seeing you again, and it's okay if you want to go and play with your other friends. Thank you for letting me pet you." She turns and runs away from me and back in the woods.

I have a pet deer.

So, cool.

"Patty, I'm coming," I call out to the forest.

Once I have the doorway open and my flashlight on, I see the momma deer standing next to her baby, watching me. "Spot, don't you come over here. If you fell into this hole, you would break your legs. Momma, take your baby away from here so she doesn't follow me." I wave at them and make a whooshing noise, hoping it scares them off from the opening.

It does.

Wow. Spot's Momma stayed by her baby's side and took her away when she saw that Spot could get hurt. I don't even have that. I have to protect myself all by myself, which is why I have to make sure no one finds this hiding place. I always have to have a place to hide.

I hang onto the flashlight as I climb back down into the dark tunnel. When the ladder sways too much, I wait for a few seconds before continuing. My feet touch down on the dirt, and I can see where I left naked Patty leaning up against the wall. I prop my flashlight against a rock, hoping it gives off enough light that I can see to put her clothes back on her. Then I brush her hair and tie the ribbon around her curls.

"There. You're all pretty and clean. I bet your owner would be happy to see that I found you and am going to take care of you. Now that I have you dressed, are you ready to explore the tunnel with me? I think you probably already know it, though, because you've been down here a long time. You don't have to be down here alone anymore; I can take care of you. No one likes to be alone. It doesn't feel good."

With Patty under one arm and the light from my flashlight leading the way, we start our adventure. I stand at the entrance and shine my flashlight in the circle of darkness that doesn't show me where it goes. Do I need to know what is in this tunnel?

"Am I going to do this?" I ask out loud. My voice echoes back to me.

Yes, I am because if this is going to be my secret place, I have to know what is in there so I'm not scared. I have to do this.

I take my first step into the exciting adventure to find out what this tunnel is all about.

I scuff along through the tunnel with Patty tucked under one arm and the flashlight in front of me, showing me the way. I move it back and forth to make sure there's nothing on either side. This tunnel is kinda creepy.

As soon as the glow leaves the spot, darkness returns. It appears the space vanishes, leaving only the area touched by light.

"Okay, Patty. We got this. We are on our first adventure together." Talking to her makes it seem like I'm not alone and helps me calm down. I move the light again to bounce off the surface—

Wait. What was that? I turn to get a better glimpse. I have to take a few more steps to the wall and lean in to see what it is.

"Sorry, Patty, but I have to put you down for a second." I lean her up against a small dirt pile.

Chapter 9
Closer

I press my face against the stone wall now, trying to get a clearer view. I squint my eyes, hoping that makes it easier to figure out what I'm looking at.

Whoa. It looks like a drawing. I trace what looks to be a head on a stick figure carved into the wall.

It looks like a child drew this—just like I did in my sluice pipe fort wall in my very first hiding place when I lived with Daddy. Back when I didn't even know what a foster child was or that I was one.

A taller stick person stands beside the first one. Is this Patty with her mommy or daddy? I have a feeling that the doll's old owner, Patty, is the one who drew this, but I'm not sure why. How long did she stay down here? I shudder for a moment when I imagine how lonely it must have been. I take a quick look back at the tunnel entrance. It's so dark here, and this is where this doll had to live for who knows how long. Then I notice the distance between the opening and where I'm standing now. Holy crap, I had no idea how far I'd walked.

"Was this your little owner, Patty?" I quickly look back up again at the drawing on the wall and notice a circle above both stick figures. I trace it. "At least your owner's Mommy is with her. I can't say that about mine. She gave me away when I was a baby." I run my finger along the rock carving of the Mommy figure. That's what it looks like to me anyway.

It looks like a sun. I would draw this, too, if I had to stay in a place like this dark tunnel all the time.

"It makes me wonder how long your owner stayed down here with you," I whisper to Patty. I shine the light down the tunnel again, hoping I can see the end this time.

"Patty, do you suppose there could be more drawings on other walls? We should find out." I hug her, and then we head toward the corner.

After I turn left, I come face-to-face with a wall made of stones and dirt. *Oh no, it can't be over already. I wanted to see how far it went.* The flashlight lights up the rocky wall as I search for any openings so I can see what's on the other side.

"Well, Patty, it seems like we're stuck. There are no openings whatsoever, and my plan is completely ruined." I walk in front of the dead end. There's a bunch of dirt around the big stones, keeping it all in place. I shine my flashlight up at the ceiling. Did this collapse, or did someone close this off on purpose? I can't tell.

I put Patty down again so I can use my hands to dig the dirt, but I can't move much of it. This thing isn't going anywhere. We are stuck.

It becomes hard for me to catch my breath. My heart pounds against my chest. I know this feeling. It happens when I'm scared and feel like I can't get away from someone hurting me.

"Well, Patty, it looks like our adventure is done. No way we are getting past this wall. I guess I'll just take you to your new home that's clean and has lots of light and other friends for you to play with. I can't wait for you to meet Raggedy and Teddy."

Right as I'm about to take off, I hear a loud *crack* coming from the other side that sounds like a sledgehammer.

Is someone stuck on that side? Is it a monster? It's not like I could see something coming at me anyway since it's so dark behind me. I hate the dark and hate it worse when it follows me like it does in this tunnel. But the idea of having a place to go to escape from someone who's hurting me is stronger than my fear right now.

Okay, I need to leave, like now.

Patty and I run down the tunnel into the big room.

The cave ended up not being bad. I thought it would be scarier than it turned out to be. At least I know that when I'm down here hanging out, nobody can get through that rock wall to hurt or find me. I'm safe down here like I was on Thunder's back in one of my old hiding places.

I spin around. "Yay, we made it. Look at the world, Patty."

I need to head home so Momma Jay doesn't start wondering where I am and comes looking for me. This hiding spot is too important for me to risk her finding it. I tuck Patty into my sweatshirt, then lift the door, then close it.

"Okay, Patty, let's go."

As I take the first step, I see my baby deer friend coming out from behind the tree.

"Hey, Spot. I wanted to see you today before I leave. I need to bring Patty back to my room without being seen, so I can't stay to pet you again. If you like, I can come to visit you tomorrow and even ask Momma Jay what I can bring that you may like to eat. 'Bye."

I look at the path. I only have a short way to go to reach my deck. I stand with Patty, looking around to make sure I don't see any wild animals that could chase me.

Go! I dash toward the house and reach my back deck in record time. I carefully take Patty out of my sweatshirt as I sit on my deck chair.

"Okay, I have to hide you under my bed until I gather enough courage to tell Momma Jay about you. But don't worry, I'll pull you out every night so you can sleep with my friends and me. I'm excited for you to meet Raggedy and Teddy, the other friends I sleep with at night." It's nice telling my doll friends what I'm thinking so I don't have to keep my thoughts inside my head.

I lean against the sliding door to make sure Momma Johnson isn't cleaning my room before I go in. The coast is clear. I hurry and put Patty under my bed. "Goodbye, Patty. I'll see you later tonight. At least you're not alone anymore. I can't tell Momma Jay about you because then I'd have to tell her where I found you. If I do that, my hiding place is gone. So, until I come up with a good lie to tell her about how I found you, I have to keep you hidden. It won't be long, I promise."

A wonderful scent drifts down the hallway from the kitchen. I go to investigate, and Momma Jay greets me with a high five and a table full of delicious food.

Yum!

I love living here.

77

***

"*Bon matin, chère.* Are ya ready for church this day?" Momma Jay is already sitting at the table sipping on her coffee as I walk out in my mouse pajamas.

"Good morning to you too, Momma Jay. Yes, I'm excited to go to church with you today. I'm glad your cold feels better, so we can go." I rub her shoulder as I stand behind her.

"Yes, *chère.* I feel a ton better. Aah happy ya can meet mey friends in church finally today. Ya can pick out what ya wanna wear as ya have plenty of clothes in de closet. We hafta leave in 'bout thirty minutes."

I sit and take a bite of my eggs and grits while Momma Jay writes on the calendar that she hangs on the fridge, reminding her what she has to do for the week. "I can't wait to visit God's house with you. This breakfast is yummy."

Momma Jay knows me well and only makes the foods I like to eat. She even makes me a hot breakfast before I leave for school.

"I'm done. Thank you for making breakfast. I'll get ready to go now. "

We arrive at the church early. That is not a surprise, as Momma Jay always plans to be early. She says being late is a sign of disrespect.

"Welcome to Bethlehem Church of God Pentecostal Church," the old man at the door, with gray hair, a beard, and chocolate skin like Momma Jay, tells me.

"Hello, Pastor Frank. Aah'd like ya to meet Anna Snow. She moved in wid mey a week ago. Dis is her first time here." She shakes his hand.

"Hello, Maude. She seems like a nice young lady."

Momma Jay rests her hand on my shoulder. "She sure is."

"Let's go, *chère,* and grab a seat."

Music circles all around us as we walk into the room with all the benches. The woman singing on stage reminds me of Ms. Lisa from my old church. Momma Jay holds the music book in her hands, and she starts to sing with the band and choir. She sounds beautiful. She can sing.

Pastor Frank walks into the room, and the music stops playing. "Welcome, everyone, and join me in an opening prayer this morning."

"Hallelujah!" I jump. I had my eyes closed, so I wasn't expecting him to slam his hand on the podium and scream at the same time. Everyone behind me starts to scream out, "In the name of Jesus. "

What's in the name of Jesus? The music starts again. Momma Jay moves to the aisle and begins to dance with her hands in the air along with everyone else. These people really love Jesus. No wonder there is a cross in my new bedroom.

"*Chère*, come join mey." Momma Jay waves her hand in the air at me. It feels really weird standing in the pew by myself, but I'm not sure that standing in the aisle with everyone dancing around me would be any better. I like to make Momma Jay happy, so I move out and stand among all the other people screaming Jesus's name and jumping around the aisle. Some of them act like they have bugs crawling all over their skin as they jerk around.

The Pastor asks everyone to take their seats after the music stops. And… like that, everyone acts normal again.

"We'd like to welcome some new members to our church service today. We will begin baptisms shortly for all of those who signed up. If you would like to be baptized in the name of Jesus Christ and be reborn today but didn't sign up, come forward." I turn to Momma Jay, who turns to face me.

"What does it mean to be reborn?"

"Getting baptized means, ya wash away der sins and allows ya t'be closer to Jesus."

"Closer to Jesus? I'd love that. He's been my friend since I was nine years old. Would he talk with me if I got baptized?"

"Well, *chère*, ya can hear him in y'all mind and heart." She whispers as she leans closer to me. But I already hear him when I need to.

Please line up now. I sit and watch as Pastor Frank prays over people, and then he dunks them in a tub of water. The people come up crying and screaming Jesus's name.

I want to be closer to Jesus. If I have to do this baptism thing to be able to do that, then that's okay. "Momma Jay?"

"*Chère*?" Her head moves closer to my face.

"I want to be closer to Jesus. Can I do this?"

"Course, *chère*. When Pastor Frank calls for others who want t'be baptized, walk out in de aisle and stand in de line." She looks happy with my question.

I'm really going to do this.

If this is what it takes to be closer to Jesus, then I'm in.

"Anyone else who wishes to be reborn, please come forward." Pastor Frank announces.

Slowly, I stand and move out of the pew.

I'm doing this. I'm really going to do this. My hands sweat as I ring them together as I walk closer to Pastor Frank.

Once I reach the altar, someone helps me walk up on stage. Whoa! I turn and see how big this church really is. People are sitting in seats close to the ceiling and more underneath. "Tell us your name?"

"Anna Snow," I whisper into the microphone.

"Do you accept Jesus Christ as your lord and savior?"

I nod.

I step over and into the little pool with Pastor Frank. His hand lays on my head. "Jesus Christ our Savior, in Your goodness and mercy, through Your Baptism, bless this child, send Your grace upon Anna Snow's head. Protect her as she goes through her life and as she walks with Your goodness and grace. Be with her in all her times of need. Show her Your love and faithfulness so that she may follow You all her days."

I'm under the water, holding my nose, as the Pastor's hand is under my back and on my Belly. This reminds me of dreams I have where I'm sinking in water but looking up. Now, I'm not sinking but rising up out of the water to people standing on their feet screaming and clapping. I wipe the water from my face quickly so I can see what's going on.

Momma Jay is in front, singing and screaming. A woman hands me a towel as I step out of the pool. "Anna, follow me. We have some spare clothes for you to wear home so you're not cold."

Once I'm changed, I head out to be with Momma Jay. She wraps her arms around me as soon as I sit down. "Repeat after me. I accept Jesus Christ as my savior." The pastor sounds like he's kinda yelling in the microphone. Everyone repeats the same words. The music starts again, and people walk to stand in front of the altar for Pastor Frank to put his hands on their heads and pray for them. Some of them act like they pass out and fall to the ground.

I've never been to a Church like this before.

Pastor Franks stops praying for everyone. We leave as the people sing on stage.

I shiver as my wet hair hits the cold September air outside. "Aah'm a proud of ya, *chère*. Jesus will always be wid ya. Y'all never be alone. He is wid ya always." Momma Jay hugs me and then opens the car door.

The engine starts, and Momma Jay quickly turns on the heat. It's a gettin' cold already. Would ya like t'grab some lunch? We can gets some spaghetti."

She is right about the weather being cold. My teeth haven't stopped banging into each other since we left the church. "Sure, I'm hungry."

This is the first time I've ever been in a restaurant that I can remember. "Good afternoon, Momma. Take a seat wherever you like." A man with a tall hat comes out to greet Momma Jay and gives her a hug. "Who's the little one with you?"

"This is Anna. She just moved in with me a little over a week ago," she says, squeezing my shoulder as her hand wraps around me.

"You're still helping us kids, I see." His big white teeth show as he winks at Momma Jay.

He bends down and is face-to-face with me. "I lived with her too when I was growing up. She helped me go to college to become a chef." He leans closer to my ear. "I was a foster kid too. We have to stick together." He stands back up.

"Ms. Anna Snow, you order whatever you like on the menu and any dessert you want too. It's on the house." He was a foster kid like me, and now he is a chef? I'm going to get out of foster care someday when I'm grown up and get a job like him. I'm never going to give my babies to foster care like Norma did, never.

"Come with me." The waitress's voice makes me jump as I'm lost in my own thoughts.

"What is a Chef Momma Jay?"

"A chef is someone who cooks good foods for de restaurant. Aah taught him how t'cook when he done lived wida mey. And now look at 'em. Dis is his restaurant. I so a proud of 'em." Her dark brown eyes look big. This is her happy look.

"Howda ya feels 'bout bein' baptized? Aah proud of ya. Jesus loves ya very much." She butters her bread, which sits in a basket on the table. I do the same.

"I love Jesus. He's been my friend for a long time. When I'm scared or afraid, I just sing *Jesus Loves Me* in my mind, and it takes me someplace else so I can get away from whatever is hurting me. So if I'm closer to him now because I got baptized in a little pool, then I'm happy 'bout that." My mouth sinks into my favorite thing, bread and butter.

"Ya right 'bout dat. Jesus can be wid ya always. Aah do whats aah can, *chère,* to keeps ya safe, so ya don't gets hurts anymore." She hits my bread with hers. I giggle.

Once we get home, Momma Jay watches an old movie while I play

81

in my room with my dolls. Then we do the same routine as we always do, including her putting braids and beads in my hair for the next day.

"Bonswa Momma Jay."

"Goodnight to ya, *chère*." I squeeze her hard as I bend down to give her a hug as she sits on the sofa.

***

"Good morning, class. Let's work on our spelling test before you head outside for recess this morning." Mrs. Song demands as she walks by my desk. She does this every morning. Sometimes she'll take the notes that other kids are passing back and forth between them while in class. One time, she even read the note out loud. Michelle is always trying to pass me notes, but I refuse to take them. I don't want Mrs. Song to read out loud what I write.

Michelle is the only friend I have in this school. No one talks to her either. So, when she is out sick or something, school sucks for me as I don't have anyone to talk to in class. The jump rope twirlers are in 5th grade. I only see them at recess, so it's good that I don't have to be alone then.

"Anna, your turn to jump in," one of the twirlers yells.

I get ready to leap when someone grabs a braid and pulls me backward.

Chapter 10
Ice Cream.

I fall onto the cement, landing hard on my back. Then, out of nowhere, someone punches me while sitting on top of me. My head swings from one side to the other with each punch.

"Get off me!" I scream. Cassie's face comes into focus. With all my might I roll over and find her on the bottom. I punch hard with my right fist and then my left. I go faster and faster and am unable to stop, that is, till someone lifts me off her.

"Knock it off, Anna!" A male teacher, who I never saw before, is holding me back as my arms are still trying to throw punches. "What the heck happened here?"

"I don't know. She just came over and started to punch me and then knocked me to the ground and jumped on top of me." Cassie cries as tears stream down her face and snot runs from her nose.

"She's a liar. She pulled me backward and then jumped on top of me and began to punch me in the face." I point to my throbbing lip. I know she drew blood because I can taste it.

A few of the snotty girls stand behind Cassie and back her story. "They are lying!" I yell as loud as I can.

"Anna isn't lying. We saw what happened. She was about to jump rope when Cassie pulled her hair, and she fell backward," the twirlers told the teacher.

"No, they are lying. We, too, saw the whole thing, and that is not how it happened." Cassie's friends yell.

"What am I supposed to believe when everyone says things happened differently? I'm going to take you to the principal and let him figure this mess out." He pulls me by my shirt as he pushes me into the office.

"Where's Cassie? She has to be in trouble, too. She did this, not me. She started it."

"Don't worry about Cassie. Worry about yourself only."

I sat in the hard wooden chair for a long time before the principal came out of his office. It's then I see Cassie walk in all by herself. She grins at me while she flings her hair. "Hello Mrs. Smith, don't you look beautiful today in your flower dress. Are you coming at the horse meeting at our house tonight to get ready for the horseshow this weekend?" She asks the lady sitting at her desk in the office.

"Why thank you, Cassie. How nice of you. I bought this dress at Ames this weekend when it was on sale. I love flowers." Cassie turns and looks at me with her eyes scrunched together. "Tell your mother to plan on me for the meeting. Have her call me if she wants me to bring something," the lady tells her. Cassie gets a huge, creepy, crooked grin and then turns to face the lady again.

"Of course I will. You have a good day."

"Ladies, step into my office, please." Cassie walks ahead of me.

We sit in chairs in front of the desk while the principal sits down behind it. "Anna, you are new to this school, and Cassie has been with us from the beginning. I find it hard to believe she started a fight with you, with this being not something she's ever done before. But I did see from your school records that you are not new to fighting or accusing people of hitting you." He glares at me. This is your time to be honest."

"I'm not lying! She pulled my hair and made me fall backward before she started punching me. Yes, I punched her back, but she took the first swing." His head moves from me to Cassie, who smiles at him.

"She's lying, and I feel bad that she lies so much, Mr. Jones. It's so sad that she does that." Cassie sounds like a grown-up the way she's talking.

"Please be quiet, Cassie, as I think about what needs to happen."

"You both are out of school for the next few days, and your parents are on your way here to pick you up. Anna, your foster mother, is also on her way.

Cassie turns her head to face me. "How sad no one wants you. But I can see why now. Maybe if you stop lying, someone will actually want you."

Every part of me wants to jump up right now and beat the crap out of her. I dig my nails into the arm of the leather chair I'm sitting in.

"That's enough, Cassie. Stop talking to her." Mr. Jones leans over the desk at her.

"Anna, your foster mother is here. Please leave my office and head home."

Cassie stands at the same time I do. "Not you, Cassie. Sit down. Your father asked me to talk with him before he arrives to pick you up."

I stand by the chair for a second, watching the both of them. "Are you and Daddy golfing together this weekend? I know how much he says that he likes to go with you to the country club?" He doesn't answer but instead turns to me.

"Head out of the office, and you'll be out for a few days."

As soon as I open the door, I see Momma Jay standing at the desk. She comes running over when she sees my face. "What de happen t'her face?" She sounds mad as she raises her voice to the lady behind the desk.

"What happened is your little foster kid beat up that sweet Cassie. That's what happened, Maude."

"I didn't start it. That Cassie girl pulled my braid and made me fall to the ground first, I swear." Momma Jay turns my head and looks at my messed-up braid.

"Dat Cassie girl is not a nice girl and dis one," she points to me as she wraps her arm around my shoulder, "woulda not do dis unless she had to." She snarled at the lady.

"Comin wid a mey, *chère*. Aah believe ya."

"She has to be out of school for a few days, Maude." The office lady snapped at Momma Jay.

"Aah believes dis child protected herself."

'Whatever you want to think, Maude."

Chère, ya out of de school for a few days. Aah dink we do ice cream each day and does a little shoppin'" She smiles at the lady and the principal who stepped out of his office in the middle of her talking.

"Aah take dis child home, but I won't punish her for stickin' up for herself." We walk out of the school with her arm around my shoulder. It felt like she was protecting me.

"Nows dat we are in de car tells me what happin'."

I give Momma Jay all the details, and I really think she believes me.

"When we getcha home, aah put somedin' on de face t'help. But now, we stop for de ice cream." She whips the car into an ice cream stand.

I eat mint chocolate chip as Momma Jay licks her strawberry ice cream cone. "Thank you for believing me," I whisper.

"Aah knows ya, *chère*. Aah does believe ya. Y'all nice girl and not de nasty girls like dat Cassie." She takes another lick.

Daddy was the last person to believe me. Now, I have Momma Jay. Maybe my life is not going to be so bad.

Momma Jay kept to her word and took me for ice cream every day that I was out of school. Now I'm sitting here staring at nothing as we talk about Math. Cassie was told that if she talked to me again, she'd be in trouble with her dad. Or at least that's what Michelle told me. The only thing I look forward to in school is jumping rope and talking with Michelle. Thank goodness today is Friday.

"Grab your things, and don't forget to do your homework this weekend."

The bell of freedom rings through the school as we all head out of the building. Momma Jay is waiting in her car. I can't get to her fast enough.

"*Mais* Friday, *chère*."

A good Friday it is. My favorite day of the week.

***

I've been sitting on a yellow pillow between Momma Jay's legs every night, watching the three funny guys on television for a few weeks now. She inspects my braids to make sure they are tight and clean, and she adds new beads.

"Grab de beads and pick out de ones y'all want t'wears *demain*."

I play with all the different beads, moving them around the

container. Momma Jay lets me do a lot of things that I want to do. She reminds me to pick out clothes that match the colors of my beads. No other foster home has let me do that. I get to pick out my own clothes and, on the weekends, I go to bed when I want to. Sometimes, it feels like a little bee sting when she braids my small hairs, but I know she's not trying to hurt me, which makes her the first foster mom not to do that.

"That braid hurt a little."

"Sorry, *chère*. Aah don't mean t'hurt ya. These small hairs are harder t'get in de braids."

I enjoy spending time with Momma Jay, and I know she doesn't mean to hurt me. She pulls the hair a little tighter, and I bite down on my lip a little bit.

"What y'all wanna do fun for de weekend?" Momma Jay asks.

I shrug. I like how the weekends are going so far, and I don't want to change anything about them. I'm so glad that tomorrow is Friday, and we only have school for a half-day. Sleeping in as much as I want on Saturdays is one reason I like weekends, thanks to Momma Jay. Sometimes, she even brings me breakfast in bed on a tray.

"I think I'da like to play outside. Dat my most favorite. If it's okay, I'd likes to take Rose an apple and Spot the old lettuce."

Momma Jay looks amused. "*Chère*, you sounded like mey."

In her language, a few words go a long way in describing things. It's so much faster than English.

"Momma Jay, I like your language. Sometimes, it's easier to speak the way you do rather than using all kinds of words to say the same thing. So yes, aah like to play outside dis weekend."

We explode with laughter at the same time. It seems like she and I tend to do that together often. She'll find something funny, and I'll laugh with her, or I'll find something funny, and she laughs with me.

"Okay, *chère*, it's time to make good doe-doe." Momma Jay hands me the brush to put in the bathroom when I get ready for bed.

"Goodnight, Momma Jay. I'll see you at breakfast." I give her a bedtime hug for the first time. After a moment, I feel her arms squeeze around me. A part of me wants to run away from her, and another part wants to stay right where I am. Her hugs feel good. I feel like she loves me like daddy did.

"Goodnight, *ma belle*. Make good doe-doe. What ya like a for breakfast in de mornin'?" I'm glad I can now understand her and don't have to ask her to repeat or explain as much. It's pretty cool how Momma Jay and I have our own language. It's she and me against the world. I don't feel so alone anymore. Momma Jay is here to help and protect me.

"Whatever ya would like to make for me is good." I stand back up.

"Okay, aah decide in de mornin' den."

"Thank you," I yell over my shoulder as I walk out of the living room and head to bed.

"Hey, Patty, Raggedy and Teddy let's go to sleep." Patty's clothes smell better, but her body doesn't—she smells just like the dusty tunnel. "Maybe I can find a way to wash your body so you smell better, like your clothes." I tuck her next to Raggedy and Teddy before talking with Jesus.

Goodnight, Jesus, and thank you for Momma Jay. She looks after me, sticks up for me with Mrs. Alex and the school, and gives me food. I don't go to bed hungry anymore. I know it's you that found her for me. I got baptized in your water in the little pool. They say that we are closer now than we were before. I'm not sure how that can happen since you've always been my best friend. But maybe now it means you're my best, best friend. Well, goodnight and I'll talk to you tomorrow.

As I lay in bed and think about Jesus, I realize something. I don't have to ask him to keep me safe anymore because he gave me Momma Jay, who will do that for him. For the first time since Jessica's house, I close my eyes and think about happy things like Momma Jay, Rose, Patty, Michelle asking me to jump rope with her and my new hiding place.

***

Recess can't come soon enough. Mrs. Song is having everyone read out loud today, and I'm hoping the bell rings before she gets to me. After recess, we always work on math which I hate too, but reading out loud sucks because I'm a horrible reader.

One person to go, and then it's my turn. Just in time, the bell rings, saving me from my nightmare of reading to everyone in the class.

"Anna Snow, hurry!" says Michelle. "We have to get to the ropes first to be able to twirl them today. We're doing double dutch!" Michelle grabs my hand and pulls me, then pushes other kids out of the way so we can get outside first. Michelle and I love to jump, but we also like to spin the ropes. We are never fast enough to get to them first. When you're spinning them, you get to decide what games you play or what song you sing in the ropes. No one has ever listened to me before, so I think it would be fun to tell them what song to sing when they are jumping. Linda and Virgina are nice, but they don't have us sing any songs when they are at work circling us.

But we're too late. Linda and Virginia are already at the ropes, spinning them in circles.

"Well, Anna, I guess we're jumping first today. Do you wanna jump together?" Michelle sounds excited.

"Sure, that sounds like fun."

"Look, girls, she's still got her Black-lady braids and beads.

"Maude Johnson is dirty."

I don't get it. Why would she say that about Momma Jay? She's a wonderful lady.

Before long, more of the kids standing around us are laughing.

Cassie continues to use words that aren't nice to Black people like Momma Jay. I don't know why she has to be so hateful, but I'm not going to let her get away with it. She's saying all these nasty things, and she doesn't even know that Momma Jay is the nicest, best foster mom I've had. Everything Cassie is saying is a lie.

Cassie pivots in front of me. She has a huge, smug grin that goes from one ear to the other. "You're nothing but a rag of nothing. No one wants you around. Look around. Everyone is laughing at you." She hisses through her teeth.

She is right. Everyone is laughing.

I warned this girl that if she ever used nasty words about me or my foster mother again, I'd break her teeth. The heat in my feet moves up to my knees and then to my hips. My stomach burns with anger like a fire pit. I clench my fist and stare back at Cassie, who plugs her nose with her fingers.

"You stink like a pig. Oink. Oink. You smell like a scu—"

My punch lands in the center of her face.

Blood gushes from Cassie's nose.

The kids standing around us scream.

Mrs. Song breaks through the circle and runs to Cassie. "What happened here?" She pulls out a tissue to stop the blood gushing from either Cassie's nose—or maybe her mouth. I don't know where it's coming from, and I don't care.

Cassie speaks while holding the tissue to her face, "That dirty girl punched me in the face." Cassie points at me while bawling like a wounded animal. I'm not sure which kind, though, because I don't know any animal that sounds like her.

Mrs. Song stands in front of me and puts a hand on my shoulder. I jerk away from her grip. "Don't touch me." I snap at her.

"Okay, Anna, but did you punch her?" Mrs. Song is standing in front of me with her face close to mine. I don't like that either. Why does she have to stand so close anyway?

When I raised my head, her eyes fixed on me. "Yep, I did." I cross my arms.

Another teacher, who I've never seen before, arrives and escorts Cassie out of the circle.

Mrs. Song turns back to me. "Anna, why did you do that?"

"Because… because Cassie was making up lies and saying mean things about people that someone should never say." I cross my arms. 'That's why!"

"Anna, that's not a reason to punch someone."

The teacher sounds kinda mad, but I don't care. If *she* called me mean, nasty words, I'd punch her, too.

I squeeze my upper arms, trying to calm down. "Mrs. Song, you'd change your mind if someone said mean things about you or your family.

Mrs. Song tried to rub my arm. I move away from her. "Actually, Anna, I wouldn't like it either. But that's not a reason to fight." I can barely hear her because she's whispering.

Mrs. Song clears her throat and then moves her hand to my shoulder. I jump out from under her grip. 'Stop touching me!"

"Fine, I won't touch you. We can't have you fighting in school, so please follow me. I'll call your foster mom to come get you."

I follow her inside. Michelle grabs my hand as she walks next to me. "Anna, that was super cool. Cassie is so mean to everyone; it's about time someone beat that girl's ass. Michelle almost trips me as she tries to give me a high-five while we're walking. We giggle for a moment as we almost fall on top of each other. "Way to go, Anna."

We all come to a halt as Mrs. Song stops walking and turns around. "Girls, there's no reason to celebrate fighting or hurting another student." She glares and crosses her arms.

I look at the pebbles on the ground rather than looking at her right now because I'm still mad. I don't agree with her. Obviously, she's not living my life because, if she was, she'd know that, to survive, sometimes you have to know how to fight. I'm sure that, in her perfect little world with her perfect mom and dad, who perfectly protected her, she never had to fight for anything. Everything was so perfect for her. So, who is she to tell me about what I should and shouldn't do to protect myself?

Once I'm in the office, the secretary tells me to grab the wooden seat by the window.

"Your foster mother will be here soon to pick you up, young lady," the principal says from behind his desk.

"Good. I don't want to stay in this school with mean kids anyway. I'm glad you called my *foster mother* to come get her *foster kid*." I stomp on the floor.

"Anna, no reason to be rude to Mr. Jones." The lady from behind the desk yells at me.

Momma Johnson enters the room. "Where y'at, *ma belle*?"

"Aah take y'all home, *chère*, we talk den." Momma Jay opens the door to leave the office.

Mr. Jones comes out of his office. "Maude, this is becoming a habit for this girl to attack another student. Something needs to be done about it."

"*Chère,* sit back down as aah handle dis." I do as she asks.

"Let mey tells ya somedin'." Momma Jay puts her hands on her hips as she takes a step toward Mr. Jones. She looks like she wants to fight him. "Get dat Cassie girl under control. She is de problem here not Anna. Aah talk wid Anna t'night de find outs what happened. Keep dat Cassie girl away from her. Got it!" I've never heard her sound as mad as she does now.

"Let's go." She taps my shoulder. "'S'okay, *chère*?" She grabs my hand and holds it as we walk out of the school.

Phew. I'm so glad she's not mad at me.

We begin to travel down the road, away from the school. "*Chère*, y'all 'k? I'm fixin' t'think de nasty girl done somedin' dat made ya angry?"

"Yes, she did. She called me and you a bad word."

Momma Jay clears her throat. "De word?"

"You wanna know the word she called us?"

She glances at me before she turns back to the road. "*Oui, chère.*"

"I don't want to say the word because I hate it. My old foster sister,

91

Lizzie, told me Black people were called this word when they were slaves."

"Slaves?" Momma Johnson's voice sounds like someone has pinched her.

"S'okay, *chère*. Aah think aah know de word ya talkin' 'bout. And y'all right; dat's nasty word. But der are other ways to stick up for de self. It's not okay t'punch someone for it, dough. Violence is not de answer to solve dings." The car pulls into the gingerbread house driveway.

"I don't like to fight Momma Jay, but I hate when people are bullies and mean to other people. It makes me so mad. I wanted to punch her as soon as she was—" I pause because my eyes are getting blurry with water. "Because she was saying mean things about you." She pats my leg before opening the car door to get out. "We talk in de house."

I follow Momma Johnson inside, then close the door behind me.

Sitting at the kitchen table, as if waiting to eat is—

Patty.

Chapter 11
Foster Family

Patty is in a chair at the table, but I don't budge an inch from the door. I fix my eyes on my new doll friend. Momma Jay must have found her. My heart pounds like a bass drum. Did I leave her lying on my mattress this morning by mistake? I think back. No, I clearly remember returning her to her place under the bed. How did she find her? I start to feel sad thinking of Momma Jay snooping through my room. This is not something she's done before. Is she starting to change now that I've lived with her for a few weeks? Is she going to start being mean now? Will she try and do girl time with me too? My mind races as I stand frozen on the wood floor. What if she makes me leave now because she knows that I didn't tell her about Patty? Any minute, I'm expecting Mrs. Alex to walk through that door and take me away to another world. I stand quiet and listen for the green monster to pull up. Nothing.

"*Chère*, come ah here. Aah wanna talk 'bout school and de doll." Mamma Johnson signals for me to move toward her by waving her hand in the air.

My mind is screaming at my feet to move. It's not working. Uh oh—-the room starts spinning just like before. The world around me becomes blurry, but I absolutely don't want to faint right now.

"*Chère?*" Momma Jay is suddenly next to me and puts a hand on my back. "Y'all 'k? Y'all face went white."

"Am I in trouble?" I ask, mumbling. The fuzzy room still spins around me slowly as if it's waiting for something.

"Nah, *chère*. I'm just fixin' to talk wid ya."

Momma Jay has a small smile on her face when I look up. I let go of the big breath I've been holding. Everything around me slows down, and I start to feel better. "How did she find my doll, and why was she looking? There has to be a reason because Momma Jay had never walked into my room before.

Taking hold of my hand, she leads me toward the kitchen table. "Take ah seat." She smiles as she points for me to sit down.

"Hey, Patty." I pick her up from the wooden chair and sit her on my lap.

Momma Johnson taps the head of my new friend. "She stinks." She plugs her nose. "De doll needs ah bath." She sounds so calm and not like how she talked to my Principal Mr. Jones.

"I know she does. I tried to wash her clothes to help the smell. But it didn't work."

"*Chère*, aah had a man comes to de house to measure rooms for carpet. Dis wood floor is stone cold in de winter. Aah wants ya to feel warm in yer bedroom. Dats when aah saw dis old doll under de bed."

"You want to put carpet in my room for me? You worry that I'll be cold in the winter?" I want to cry, and I'm not sure why. It's not like she's hurting me. Why do I want to cry right now, and why do I feel like I can't stop it from happening? I swallow hard over and over again to stop my tears. None of this makes sense. Why do I want to cry right now when nothing is wrong, and I'm not hurt?

"Yes. Aah don't wants ya feet t'be cold dis winter." She tilts her head to the side. "Does ya dink aah snooping in yer room?" She leans closer to me.

"Yeah," I whisper.

"Oh, *chère*, aah sorry aah didn't mention it to ya. Aah make sures in de futures aah tells ya when aah needin' t'go into ya room." She shakes her head. "Aah sorry." She looks sad.

I clear my throat because it feels like a nut is stuck in it from trying to hold back my tears. "That's okay. I understand." I'm so relieved. This sounds like Momma Jay, and maybe she isn't really changing.

"*Chère*, where de doll comes from?" She leans back away from me and sits up in her chair at the kitchen table. "Y'all not in trouble. I'm just curious 'bout de doll. She looks and smells old."

I'm thinking about letting Momma Jay know about my hiding place. I haven't had to use it here since I'm not in any danger or trouble. Maybe I don't need it. It's possible that I can tell her. I don't want to lie to her when she's been so kind to me. She even moved her bedroom and is going to put carpet in the room so my feet are warm.

I don't want to lie to Momma Jay. And... I'm not going to.

"Anna?" She never calls me by my name. She sounds worried.

"Um... I... um... found her... in the... um... underground tunnel." Momma Jay's eyes bulge. "A *tunnel*?"

"Over by the trees, there's a secret passage in the yard. When I opened the door, I climbed down a ladder that was attached to the wall. I found an enormous room in the ground that looked like somebody had made it out of dirt. And there's a tunnel at the end of it. I went in it and found Patty, leaning against the wall all by herself. I felt sad for her, so I brought her home."

Momma Jay moves closer and touches Patty's ringlets. "Y'all did a good job on her hair." She touches Patty's head and then rubs her shoulder. "Why y'all name her Patty?"

"'Cause of this." I lift Patty's shirt to show Momma Jay the mark sewn into Patty's fabric skin over her heart. "See? It says Patty. So, I guess that's her name. Or maybe it's the name of the girl who owned her and left her behind.

"Oh my!" Momma Jay covers her mouth. "Dis doll is verra old." She traces the letters. "Aah don't think dis is thread, but knows what ita be." Momma Jay stands up and then pushes into her chair. "Let's go so y'all can show mey 'bout de tunnel."

We let the screen door slam shut as we leave the house. We make our way through the woods to the opening of my underground world.

I stoop to lift the door.

"*Chère*, y'all be careful."

"I am." The door swings open just as it always does, then falls to the ground. I move closer to the opening, and, this time, I wave Momma Jay to come closer so she can see.

"*Chère*, it'sa dark down der." She steps away from the opening.

95

"Would you like to come with me to see the room and the cave?"

Momma Johnson points to the rickety old ladder on the wall. "Nah *chère*. De ladder won't hold mey's weight." With a giggle, she traces her hands down her body.

I chuckle as she does a little dance. "In the cave where I found Patty, I also saw carvings of stick figures on the wall. I'm wondering if the person who owns Patty is the one who drew them."

Momma Jay rubs her chin as she watches me. "I wonder if dis was part of de tunnels in de undergrown railroad dat freed slaves." Momma Johnson takes another step to get nearer the dark hole. She holds my hand. "Y'all found ah stick drawin' in de wall?"

"Yes. I saw a small stick drawing of a girl, with a bigger one standing next to her, and their hands touching each other. Could that be Patty with her momma? It's kind of like what we're doing right now." I swing her hand with mine.

She winks at me.

There's something special about holding her hand that I enjoy. I really like her, and I know she cares about me.

"Uh... Momma Jay? Would it, ah, be okay if I... call you Momma instead of Momma Jay?" My voice is quiet. I think a real Momma who cares about her kids would act just like Momma Jay. I want her to be my Momma like she was the chef at the restaurant where we ate spaghetti. He was a foster kid, too, but he lived with Momma Jay till he went to college. He called her Momma. That's what I want, a Momma.

It's too late for me to take back what I said. Suppose she says no? I'd feel incredibly stupid. Why did I even ask her in the first place? No one has wanted to be my Momma so far; what made me think she did? Just because she was nice to me? What if...

Momma Jay takes a step back and gently pulls my hand to join her. "*Chère*, aah *love* for y'all to call mey Momma. Aay be happy."

She wraps her arms around both of us. Just like the girl in those mysterious cave drawings, I have a momma who will always be here to hold my hand and keep me safe.

"Momma?"

She lets go of our hug and looks at my face.

"What's the underground railroad, and what does it have to do with Patty and slaves?

"Mais, *chère*, tunnels like dis one was for de Black peoples to run

96

through to get free in de north. Patty might be from a slave girl 'cause she de old lookin'. The girl mighta run fast and drop her doll. Maybe de Inez family helped de slaves since dis here tunnel is on de property dat Nellie Inez told mey has been in der family from de start of time."

"I'll ask Ms. Nellie Inez when I see her to see if that's what the tunnel was for."

"Dat a good ah idea. "But, *chère*, y'all promise mey dat y'all see all peoples for who de ares and not de color of der skins, no madder where y'all live."

She holds up her pinky finger. I know what this means. We lock them together.

In every foster home, I learn something different. With Daddy, I learned all about cars. With Sue and Allen, I learned about horses. With Jessica and her husband, I learned how to speak proper English, as she liked to call it. And now, here with Momma, I learned that I will never be mean on purpose to hurt someone no matter what they look like. Momma's giggling interrupts my thoughts.

"T'fight racism and ignorance, y'all need t'use de smarts." She points to my head and then my hands. "Not de fist. Change de the way peoples dink. Dats how t'change dings, no matter what t'is 'bout."

I hug her. I can't stop the tear that falls down my cheek onto her chest. "I'm sorry your people were slaves. I'm so sorry." I don't like to hear about people that I love getting hurt. It makes me sad.

"*Chère* why y'all sniffles." She steps back. Her hand gently touches my cheek. "Y'all a strong girl. And a carin' one, too." She lifts my chin so that I'm looking up at her. Then hugs me again. I hang onto her and don't let go.

"Now, let's talk 'bout de fightin' in de school." Momma steps out of the hug. "Fightin' don't fix racism. But if y'all has to do it t'protect de self, dat different." For a moment, Momma adjusts one of my braids to keep it away from my face as we move back from the hole. "So did ya fight t'protect de self or did ya fight for de racism slang?"

As I stand here holding her hand once more, I realize it's time for me to admit the truth and not just come up with something to make hitting Cassie okay. It's hard for me because I feel as though she deserved to be punched. It's not as if the Cassie girl was hurting *me* with her fist. The only thing I had a problem with was her words. Did I have the option to act like she wasn't there? I didn't want to. I wanted to shut up her nasty mouth. As I search for the right answer, Momma's eyes never leave my face.

"The reason I punched her square in the face was because of the words she was using. But I don't want to ignore it." I look down at the ground and away from Momma. "I guess I should have used my brain and not my fist. I could have told her that I felt bad for her because she was stupid." Momma chuckles.

"Y'all right, de girl's actions are stupid. But what ya say instead 'member outsmarts de girl wid yer brains." She taps my head.

"I could have told her that I felt bad for her because she's mean and then walked away." Momma claps. "Yes. Dat's using de brains."

I *know* I won't be able to walk away from that; it will be hard for me. When I have a hard time with something I used to only pray to Jesus for the answers so I can do that. But now he gave me Momma too. "What should I do when I see her in school?"

"Instead of punchin' de girl, y'all can tell her dat y'all feel sad for her, and y'all hope dat, someday, she can be ah nice girl instead of a nasty one. Try de words, not de fist." She pats my shoulder. "Try stayin' away from de nasty Cassie girl next time y'all's at de school." She winks, this time with both eyes while saying, "'K?"

"Okay, I'll stay away from Cassie. Am I allowed to take Patty back to her friends in my room?"

"Sure, y'all can do dat. Let's close dis door first. Y'all can does what ya wants dis weekend as aah no plans. But aah asks y'all t'please lemme know if ya go to de underground tunnel. Aah wanna makes sure aah knows when y'all down der."

I nod.

"Good, *chère*." She claps. I wonder if her hands get red because she claps all the time when she's happy.

I take Patty back to my bedroom and place her on my mattress next to Raggedy and Teddy. "Well, Patty, I have fantastic news. I can finally stop hiding you. So, now, you don't have to be alone under my bed. You have a new family now with Momma Jay and I. We are like your foster family. But don't worry, we'll be a nice one.

***

"Please write September 19th on all your papers today." Mrs. Song instructs all of us.

What? Today is September 19th?

98

Chapter 12
Another Car Ride

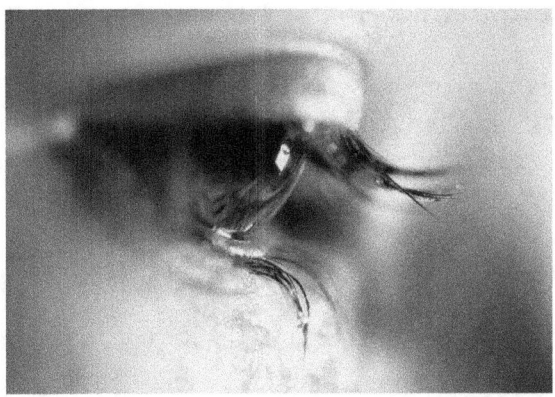

September 19th is an important date for me because it's the day I celebrate my birthday. The teacher I'd had when I'd been in my first foster home, Mrs. Young, was the one who gave me that date. Since I didn't know my actual birthday, she'd created that day for me to celebrate in class like the other kids. She'd even brought in cupcakes for me to pass out. So now, unless someone tells me my real birthdate, that's the one I use.

I should let Momma know that today is my birthday. I bet she would do something fun, like make me some yummy food. She might even surprise me with a homemade cake. *Today is my special day. Happy birthday to me! I'm ten years old*, I sing to myself in my head.

"Class, time for math. Remember to have your books out and work quietly at your desk."

I'd rather think about my big day than how many apples Johnny has after he accidentally dumped some out, picks up new ones, and then eats three of them. Why is it important for me to know how many apples are left? Can I just say there are apples left? Is that what really matters? Why do I have to know the exact number? As long as he has apples, he won't go hungry. That's the important thing to remember. Going to bed hungry hurts. Mother and Mrs. Dorsey made me go to bed all the time without food. I hate that feeling.

The classroom door opens, and the principal's head appears. "Can you please ask Anna to make an office trip and bring all her belongings? She's leaving school today."

Mrs. Song's voice fills the entire classroom as she directs me to collect my things and make my way to the office. I become the center of attention as my classmates chant, "Ooh, ooh, Anna's in trouble," while they laugh at me.

Why does everyone in school always laugh at me? I never know why. I'd fix it if I could. I really, really don't like people laughing at me, and if I could make them stop, I would. But someone has to tell me *why* they're laughing so I know what to do.

Michelle gives me a high five as I leave.

"I'll catch up with you tomorrow and we can jump rope," I say to her.

The door slams with a *bang* behind me. What the heck is going on? Has something happened to Momma? Is that why I'm being asked to leave sooner? Did—

Mrs. Alex.

She's standing in the office.

Please, no. No. No. I won't let her take me away again! I love Momma, and I'm happy for the first time since leaving Daddy.

A book slips from my hands and slams onto the hallway floor. I run toward the exit, hoping to run back to my secret hiding place and never see Mrs. Alex again.

I run *right* into the principal.

"Mrs. Alexander was concerned that you might try to escape. That is *not* acceptable." He sounds mad at me. Mr. Jones guides me to my caseworker, holding onto my arm.

"Anna's leaving today. I'll provide instructions about where to send her records. I appreciate your help."

The lady behind the desk acts all nice to Mrs. Alex but I know she's not. "Of course. I'll make sure I get everything around and send it over to the new school."

At the top of my lungs, I shout, "I want to stay with Momma! I can't stand you, Mrs. Alex! I can't stand you!"

She shakes her head and sighs. "Look, Anna, if it becomes necessary, I will call the police. You can choose to come with me or go with them. Choosing me would make things a lot easier for you."

"Fine! Call the police. I don't care! I want to see Momma and at least say goodbye to her." I hate to beg, but I don't want Momma to think I left her willingly. "Mrs. Alex, *please* let me have a moment to say goodbye to Momma."

"Let's go, Anna. We can talk in the car." She puts her hands on my shoulder and steers me out, leaving me no choice.

Principal Jones walks behind us, probably to make sure I don't try to run again.

I seriously want to.

And then I see that hideous green car just sitting there, mocking me.

I really don't want to get in, but I also don't want to go to the police.

I climb onto the icy leather seat, and the door slams shut, and once again, I'm sitting in the rear seat next to my garbage bag, Raggedy, and Teddy.

"Do you know where Patty is?" I ask. I hate having to ask her for *any*thing, but I don't want to leave my new friend behind—I have very few as it is, and I'm her foster mother.

Mrs. Alex looks at me in her review mirror. "Who's Patty?"

"The doll—the one I rescued from—" No. I'm not going to mention my hiding place. Mrs. Alex can't know I find them at new homes. "She's a doll I found in the woods. She's not here with the others. I hope you didn't drop her when you were carrying my stuff to the car. That's what happened with my brother's teddy bear, which is why I have him now."

"Oh, the black, old doll? The thing smelled terrible and was likely infested with bugs. I put it in the garbage can at Maude Johnson's. There's no need to bring it to your next foster placement."

It's surprising how calm she sounds, considering she just threw Patty *away*. But then, since she's so used to tossing me at different houses, I guess she's used to throwing things away. I certainly feel like her unwanted trash. She makes me move in garbage bags, or at least she doesn't stop the foster parents from doing it. Then—she dumps me off at a new home just like daddy used to take the garbage to the dump. Foster parents just get rid of me when they don't want me anymore, just like they throw out trash.

"*You're* the bug, and you drive a nasty green car!" I yell because there's not much else I can do. I can't get out, and kicking the back of the seat doesn't stop her.

Clutching Teddy, I bury my head into his fur and let my tears fall in silence. Teddy becomes as wet as my face in a short time.

Mrs. Alex drives past trees, houses, stores, and buildings—one more world that I'm leaving behind.

"Why do I have to leave? Huh? Why?"

"Anna, I'm not always able to tell you everything, and this is one of those times. I can't tell you why you had to leave." She turns her mirror in my direction.

"You have to tell me. I want to know why. I have to know why!" I yell.

"Yelling isn't going to get me to tell you the answer to that question. I'm sorry, Anna, I didn't want to see you move again either. Maude Johnson is a nice lady. But this was out of my control?"

"Mrs. Alex, what do you mean it was out of your control? Why did you make me leave? Answer the question."

"I'm sorry, Anna, I cannot do that. Please sit back as we have a little road trip ahead of us."

Of course we do. She says that all the time on these damn trips. I grind my teeth together.

I bury my face into Teddy.

Goodbye, Momma. You mean a lot to me, and I love you. I will always hold you in my heart. I know you didn't do this to me. I don't know how I know that. I just do. I touch the new beads and braids she put in my hair last night. I'll miss those times with her. Another tear finds its way to my mouth.

I'm sorry, Patty. I know I promise to keep you, but I had no choice. When Momma comes across you in the trash, she'll rescue you and look after you. She will one hundred percent do that for both of us.

Bye, Michelle. I loved skipping rope together with you.

Goodbye, Rose. I wish you plenty more apples.

Miss Nellie Inez, thank you for your kindness and for sharing stories about your granddaughter and horse with me.

Goodbye, this nice new world. I hate that I won't see you again.

My body trembles, and my throat burns as I struggle to hold back some of my tears. I finally found Momma and felt safe. Mrs. Alex just took that from me, just like she took Curtis from me. She doesn't want me to be happy.

Before too long into the trip, the vehicle stops. I don't move. I don't want to open my eyes since I have no idea what's going to happen to me in the next home. Not everyone will be like Momma, I know. No one has so far. I don't want to see this new world that Mrs. Alex is taking me to.

The car engine dies as Mrs. Alex turns it off.

That's how I'm feeling right now—I'm dying. I'm dying inside with each move.

Chapter 13
Garbage

Mrs. Alex's car door slams. It won't be long before she demands that I get out of the vehicle with my stuff, probably within seconds. My door opens. "Would you like some food? We have a short trip ahead, and you might start to feel hungry, as it will be a while before we arrive at your new family."

I shut my eyes tightly and press against Teddy. I choose to do and say absolutely nothing.

"Anna? Do you want something to eat?" Mrs. Alex stands next to the automobile; I assume because I don't lift my head to look at her. With a thunderous crack, she forcefully closes the car door.

How much time does it take for this woman to understand? Eating French fries with her is completely out of the question for me. I close my eyes and nuzzle into Teddy.

Curtis! I leap up and eagerly scan the back cushion for any hidden message left by my brother. If Mrs. Alex moved him to a new foster home, he'd be back here for sure and would leave me a note hidden somewhere. Despite digging into the cracks of the seat, I find nothing.

Maybe my brother found a nice family where he can stay put and be happy, unlike me, who keeps moving around. I hope that's the case.

As the door opens, the scent of fries fills the air. Mrs. Alex was right. I'm feeling like I could eat something because she took me before lunch. A loud rumbling sound comes from my stomach.

"I heard your stomach growl. Anna." Mrs. Alex is talking like she cares about me, "I know you didn't get a chance to eat before we left your school. Would you like some of my fries?" She reaches over the seat and tries to hand me a fry.

"Nope. I want nothing from you." Facing me, she turns her body in the driver's seat.

"Anna. I wish I could have taken you to say goodbye to Maude Johnson, but foster care doesn't operate that way. Believe me, this was the easiest option for you. Going back to see her would only have made the transition harder." Her voice sounds soft and kind. I raise my head from Teddy and glance at her.

"My apologies for not bringing Patty. I was unaware of how much she meant to you. Though she really smelled like she was a thousand years old." It's obvious that Mrs. Alex is making an effort to talk to me. It's not going to work. Talking nicely to her is something I will never do. Never!

Finally, after she realizes that I'll stare at her but say nothing and I won't take her gross fries, she turns back around to bring the green beast to life by turning on the engine. I bury my head in Teddy's belly to escape this painful ride and my life.

"Get ready, Anna. We're in for a long trip ahead. We don't need you trying to run back to Maude Johnson."

Now she's back to being the mean, wicked witch she is.

***

"Momma, this is the best Po'boy that you've made so far."

"Aah glad y'all likes it. Remember, *chère*, y'all de good ah girls, and don't ya lets de peoples tell y'all anythin' differ…"

"Anna, wake up! We've arrived."

I had a dream about Momma. A tear slowly makes its way down my face. There's pressure on my shoulder. "Anna, it's time to wake up." Mrs. Alex leaned into the back seat and over me inside the automobile. "You were out, kid." She smiles.

Using Teddy's big puffy belly, I turn away from her. "Anna, we have to get out of the car," she sounds urgent. Gather your belongings and join me at the door. The clock is ticking, so let's hurry up and get going."

Of course she doesn't have a lot of time. Of course, time is running out for her. She never stays long when she moves me.

Hurry up. I've got things to get done, and I've got to get going. She says the same old crap, just in a different place.

My new foster mother is standing on the front porch of an old, small, yellow house. The house is so close to the road, it's a wonder a car has never driven through it. I roll down my window so I can hear what they are saying to each other.

"It may take Anna a second to get out of the car; she's having a hard time. Maude Johnson and she were close, but Anna's mother, Norma, requested that we transfer Anna to a white family because Maude is African-American."

What? Why does Norma get to decide where I live? I don't even know her and never met her. And Momma was not African-American— she told me she is Louisiana French Creole. Like always, Mrs. Alex has no clue what she's talking about.

"She'll get over it before too long," the medium-sized woman with long, black hair says to Mrs. Alex and looks at me in the car.

We lock eyes for a second. My stomach hurts really bad, and I have no idea why, but I have a terrible feeling about this foster mother. I don't look away; I glare right at her 'til she turns back to Mrs. Alex again.

"Does she have behavioral problems?" my new foster mother asks.

What exactly does *behavioral problems* mean?

"I guess she could. She likes to run away at times." She glances at me, watching her, and then clears her throat. "I've had to call the police before to help me move her."

Nice, Mrs. Alex. Tell her all the horrible things about me. Don't forget to mention how awful my birth mother, Norma, is.

As if she can hear my thoughts, Mrs. Alex tells whatever-this-lady's-name-is the same story about Norma that she's told all my foster families in the past.

Before heading to Nashville to record a record, Norma left her children in the care of her friend. Six months later, she came back and insisted on having the children returned to her care. Several months

106

passed, and Norma sold the children to her brother-in-law, Anna's father, in exchange for drug money. Anna has multiple hospital reports documenting abuse, including cigarette burns, possible sexual abuse, and other injuries caused by Anna being thrown across the room to test if she could land on the sofa. According to reports, this was a drinking game. It's dangerous for the kids to be unsupervised with Norma. Norma engaged in prostitution, exchanging sex for money, whatever that entailed...

I bury my head back into Teddy, trying to make Mrs. Alex's voice disappear. Why doesn't Mrs. Alex just make it easy and tell her that Norma is crap, and she can't take care of me? I don't believe all the things she says about Norma. I think Mrs. Alex is making it all up so she can keep me in foster care.

Then, just like before, this new world and their voices fade.

I wake up to Mrs. Alex's voice booming at me through the window.

"Let's go! It's time to get out of the vehicle. Mrs. Kray is waiting to meet you." Mrs. Alex yanks Teddy out from under me, causing my head to hit the seat. "Come on, Anna. Move it along. Mrs. Kray has all the information she needs, so you're all set."

I do as she directs and grab my garbage bag and Dolly. After I exit the car, I yank Teddy back from her. "Give me my brother's bear and leave me alone."

Mrs. Alex's vehicle starts just as my garbage bag scrapes against the rocks. Where is she going? Isn't she even planning to walk me into this house?

Right when I spin around to see what's up, Mrs. Alex drives off and waves goodbye through the window.

I am alone in the middle of the driveway. What do I do? I could drop everything and run away with Raggedy and Teddy, but I think they would slow me down.

As I turn around to explore my options, I'm startled by a voice shouting at me from the porch.

"Anna, let's get in the house! I don't want to call the police on you already for thinking about running away. Mrs. Alexander told me that you're a runner." She has a high-pitched voice that is seriously annoying.

I'm already worried before I even get to know her. I have a gut feeling that this lady doesn't like foster kids and I don't think this is going to turn out good for me.

I do what I'm told and reach the porch. A tall lady with short blonde curly hair is standing on the porch with her hand in front of her for me to shake. Perfect. I plan to make it clear to this woman that I mean business, and I'm not scared.

I carefully set Raggedy down and give this woman my firm grip, just as Daddy taught me.

"Ouch. Be careful, child." She glares at me.

"I'm not a child. My name is Anna. Please call me that and not *child*." I grip her hand tightly.

"Feel free to call me Georgia, and I can address you however I please." She tightens her hold.

My hand aches, but I'm not going to cry, and I won't let go—even as she squeezes harder. I never quit. To be a foster kid, you always have to fight back. Not quitting something is fighting back.

"Georgia," some guy says from inside, "who's here?" He sounds gruff.

"Our new foster child." Oh, sure, she sounds nice to *him*.

The look she gives me that he can't see is anything *but* nice. "Gather your belongings and come inside the house. Keep quiet because Frank doesn't like a lot of noise. You'll face consequences if you're too loud." Georgia gives my hand one more squeeze before she lets go.

I pull my trash bag across the door, causing it to scrape against the worn, wooden floor.

"Pick that garbage up, young lady. I don't want my floors scratched." She talks through her teeth like Mother used to do when she was mad at me. Great. Please don't let her act like Mother. The bag is too heavy and taller than me, making it impossible for me to lift.

"Well, well, who do we have here?" A man with glasses and a round body, who's holding a newspaper, walks up to me and says, "Hello, Anna. Welcome to our house," before disappearing into another room.

"Grab your stuff and head up the stairs." Georgia points into the living room through an archway. The staircase runs up along the side of the wall in the living room.

I don't—*can't*—move. I look around. I have a bad feeling about this foster mother. She already reminds me of Mother, and that is not good. Georgia starts to walk toward me, so I stand still to see if she wants something from me.

"Why are you still standing there? Get moving, child. You need to unpack and get back down here when the boys get home from school, which is soon."

B... boys? The entire room starts rotating, making everything blur together. I can feel my legs turning to jelly, and I know what that means. I'm about to black out again. Oh no, not—

Someone is slapping my face. "Wake up, child, and get going. We can't do this all day."

A splash of water hits me, and I jerk up into a sitting position.

She's standing before me with an empty glass.

"What the heck was that?" I brush water out of my eyes.

Georgia bends down, and, out of nowhere, she smacks me across the face. "I won't tolerate swearing or disrespectful talk in this house, got it? Get your smart little self up those stairs now," my new foster mother says with a scratchy voice. I wonder if she smokes like Mother did. They even sound alike.

I struggle to stand as the area continues to spin around me. I fight to take one step at a time. I can't believe she threw water on me. I catch myself as I start to lean to the right and then to the left. I stop and close my eyes just for a second so the room stops spinning. Carrying my garbage bag, Teddy, and Raggedy, I drag my feet toward the staircase. One step at a time, I climb to the second floor. I'm lost and don't know which bedroom is mine, so I go through each room in the hallway.

I stumble upon a room with two sets of bunk beds with boy-smelling clothes lying everywhere. My legs start to shake. I stand in the doorway. It smells like Derek in here. I start to gag at the thought. *Don't throw up in here, Anna. Georgia threw water on you when you passed out. What do you think she'd do if you threw up?* I don't want to live with boys again.

I need to keep moving and get away from this room before I vomit and get myself in more trouble.

The next thing I come across is the bathroom, followed by a tiny room at the end of the hallway with only a bed that looks like a cot.

Guess I found my place. No comfy princess bed for me here, I guess.

I set my bag on the floor and place Raggedy and Teddy on the small bed. I sit and hold Raggedy. "This is our new home, and I don't think it's going to be a good one. Maybe we won't have to stay here too long." I wrap my arms around her and cry into her chest.

Jesus, I'm scared. Why don't I have a normal life? Why couldn't I stay with Momma? Why can't I have a real mom and dad who love me? Why is all this happening? Why me?

"Anna, come downstairs."

Georgia's voice outside my room jolts me awake.

Darn. It's so much nicer in my dreams.

I drag myself off the cot and head out.

"Who's the new kid?" some older boy asks.

"Seriously, Mom? We got a girl this time? Girls are gross. Why couldn't it be another boy?" another guy asks, and he sounds older than the last one.

Are they the same age as Derek?

Are they just like Derek?

Forget my bad feelings about this woman; I don't like the idea of these two boys at all.

"We don't need any more male presence in this house, and I'm the only girl, so I thought it'd be nice to have another female. Plus, Clay, you have no say. This is my house, so hush up and go find something to do while I set the table for dinner."

Georgia is talking with someone just as I reach the top of the stairs.

"Mom, do you and Dad really need another mouth to feed right now? I just started working and can help out with food and stuff."

"Thanks, Brad, but we can manage. Having Anna here brings in money that can help since I lost my job. So, no need for you to take care of your father and me. You have an apartment and your own bills to worry about." Georgia sounds nice talking with him. That's not how she talks to me. She has talked grumpy to me the entire time I've been here so far. She's talked nice to Frank and now to one of her kids.

"Whatever, Mom."

My hands start shaking. He sounds like Derek.

That's not Derek. I heard her say, Brad. *He is not Derek. This is your mind playing tricks on you, Anna.*

"Cut it out, Brad. You don't live here anymore. Move out of the way so I can throw the ball."

"Shut up, Clay. Just throw it already."

Right when I take my last step, a football crashes into my face.

"Ouch. That hurts." In an instant, the entire room is filled with stars all around me. My hand rubs my cheek and the side of my face. I think they meant to hit me on purpose because, so far, none of them have tried to be nice to me.

"What the hell, fellas? Remember when I told you not to throw the ball inside the house?" So, it's okay for her to talk like she wants to, but not me. Yup, she's Mother.

Georgia shouts at both of them but never bothers to check on me.

"Yes, we remember, but we wanted to throw it anyway." They both start laughing at her.

Georgia pushes her teeth together along with her eyebrows. "You won't find that funny in a second. Remember who the hell you're talking to, or you'll both regret it. Trust me."

Whatever she would do to them made both of them stop immediately. They have a scared look on their faces as they turn their heads away from her. I wonder why they would regret it. What would she do to them? Maybe I don't want to know. I have to keep quiet here so I don't get into trouble or draw too much attention to myself. This is a foster mother I better not mess with.

"Anna, make sure you move so the ball doesn't hit you next time." She turns her back to walk away from us.

Next time? There's going to be a next time? I thought she told them not to throw the ball in the house. Can they do whatever they want? Boy, if I'd ever done something after Mother specifically told me not to, it was hands in the hot water for me. But these guys don't seem to worry about it. Yet *I'm* the one who gets hit and water thrown on her for something I can't control. What is *with* this woman? I make a fist.

"It's a little late for that, don'tcha think?" I snap back.

As Georgia turns toward me, everyone in the room stops talking. This woman is being mean to me for no reason, and I've got to do something to stick up for myself. I have to remember what Momma said, "use de smarts, not de fists."

"Will there be a next time? You just saw them hit me in the face. That's not okay." I try to calm the anger raging inside of me.

"Whoa, Brad. Did you hear how the foster girl just told Mom off?"

Everyone's eyes were on her, waiting to see Georgia's next move.

I stand there with my hand on my cheek.

Georgia slowly walks up to me and then stands in front of me.

She smacks me across the face—on the same side the football had hit. "Child, watch your word choice in this household. Next time, it will be a lot harder. Head back to your room and get comfortable. I'll give you a call when it's time to eat."

"I'm not afraid of you," I grit out as I glare right back at her.

Her mouth forms a circle. "*What* did you say to me?" She leans closer.

I don't move.

This reminds me of the time I stood in front of Mrs. Dorsey and let her hit me—'til she knocked me out. I don't want that to happen again, but I will *not* be afraid of this nasty woman, and I won't ever let her think I am. But maybe, now, with all the boys standing next to her, it's not the time to show her how strong I am because I don't know what they'll do, and I *really* don't want them to do to me what Derek did.

"Do you want me to take care of this, Mom?" Brad asks her.

Take care of this? How? Like Derek?

Yeah, maybe I should just back down until it's just her and me. The boys make the odds all wrong.

"I got it, Brad. Go and help your father outside and let him know that dinner will be ready soon." Georgia never moves her gaze off me.

Despite what I'd just decided, neither do I.

But slowly, I do take a few steps backward toward the staircase. I'm still staring right at her, but when my ankle bangs into the bottom step, I turn around and head up the stairs. I turn back when I reach the top.

Georgia doesn't move from her spot. I move to stand against the wall around the corner so I can hear what's happening, but she can't see me. I want to know what she says about me and if she tells someone what she might do to me later.

"Mommy, what happened to that girl? Why can't she play with me?"

It's a little kid's voice that I haven't met yet. Or at least I don't remember seeing one.

"Kevin, the new girl, is bad and needs to be punished, so she has to go to her room." Her nice voice is back. Why have me here to live if she doesn't like me? That doesn't make any sense to me. "Go outside and have fun with your toys." Kevin must've listened to her as I hear footsteps run away.

I arrive at my room and lie down on my bed with my trusty Raggedy.

Why me? Is this what my life will look like? Will Georgia act like Mrs. Dorsey or like Mother did in my old foster home? I put my hand to my cheek, remembering the slap.

Why me? Why is this my life?

I grab Raggedy and cry again into her chest. My life of happiness is gone and replaced by a new nightmare called Georgia. This can't be real. How can there be so many mean people in this world who like to hurt kids? What is going to happen to me here?

Before I know it, Georgia is standing at my door. "Wake up, It's mealtime. Join us downstairs to meet everyone."

I stand up with Raggedy.

"Leave that old doll on the bed." She strolls over and plays with my braids. "We'll get these nasty things outta your hair tonight. You're not black; you're a white girl, so you should look like one." She heads back down the hallway toward the stairs.

Reaching up, I play with my hair and beads. I want to keep them in. I wish I were French Creole like Momma because then I wouldn't have had to leave and be with this nasty woman. If only I could find my way back to my hidden underground railroad cave. If I could get back to that tunnel, no one would find me, and just like it had helped Patty's momma find freedom, maybe I could, too. But since I can't get back there, I need to look around fast. I definitely think I'm going to need a place to hide from Georgia.

When I can, I'll have to check out things around here to see if I can find another hiding place.

But, since I don't have one now, and I really don't want to get hit again, I head downstairs. I'll try not to get smacked again—

Oh no.

The smell in the dining room stops me. Is that? Did she make?

Oh, man. This is going to be worse than I thought.

Chapter 14
An Old Castle

There's no seat for me at the table.

Why am I even surprised? It's not like this woman has even pretended to be glad I'm here. "Where do *I* sit?" I ask as I stand next to the big table. Everyone turns and looks at me. It's like I'm standing in front of the classroom again. Georgia doesn't do anything at first except take a bite of the nasty stuff on her plate.

"Georgia? Where do ya want me to sit?" I ask again.

"First sound a little like your smart and not say *ya*. The correct word is *you*. Second hold on and I'll find you something." I hold on okay as seconds turned into minutes. I think she just likes making me stand there. I'm beginning to hate this woman already.

Georgia stands up like she is in slow motion and moves a small desk next to the large table. The stool has no back, and the small table looks like an old-fashioned desk. "Unfortunately, we can't fit another person, so you can sit here and feel like you're sitting with us."

She smiles at me as if I should be oh-so-grateful, but I get the feeling that sitting here all by myself might make her happy. Like she wants me to know I'm not good enough for them.

Well, I have a surprise for her. She's not the first person to try to treat me that way. But at least I know that I'm not a nasty person like her. Like Momma said, "member ya a goods girl." That's who I am, no matter what Georgia does to me. She's not going to break me. I'm strong. I'm Anna Snow.

Big deal. They don't want to include me in their family; I don't care. I hope I can leave soon anyway—especially because she made the stupid ham and cabbage I hate. I can't believe I didn't even notice it when I walked in. Of course, that might be because she'd smacked me. Maybe I *should* try to eat some because it will, for sure, make me throw up. That would show her.

But I do *not* want to get slapped in the face again, and throwing up all over their dining room won't make a good impression either.

"Uh, Georgia? I have an allergy to cabbage. It makes me sick." Our eyes meet as she looks in my direction.

"*Allergic?* The caseworker said you don't have any allergies." My new foster mother looks confused. "Did Mrs. Alex know about your allergy?"

"I have no idea what she knows. She claims to know everything about my life, but she's wrong." I cross my arms.

"Anna, there's absolutely no excuse for your snotty and rude behavior toward Mrs. Alex. She has many children to look after, and you're just one of them." Her eyes squint closer together, and her mouth spreads across her face higher on one side than the other.

I shrug. "I don't care what she has."

Georgia studies me while everyone passes the food around the table. "If you're not hungry, why not make a peanut butter sandwich and go play outside? There's no need for you to sit and watch us eat." A bunch of that gross stuff lands on a plate with a *plop*.

Gross.

I avoid smiling, afraid she might rethink that offer. Instead, I pretend to be upset. "Okay, Georgia, I'll go do that." Even though I'm thrilled about this, I'm working hard to make my voice sound quiet and sad. I love peanut butter, and the chance to get away from her is like icing on a cupcake.

I go into the kitchen, open each drawer to find what I need, then make my sandwich. I load it up with lots of peanut butter and jelly, then head back through the dining room.

"Anna," Georgia says, "go out the back door of the kitchen. There's no need to pass through this room to get outdoors."

I spin in a circle and search for the door in the kitchen. I don't want to ask her because I might give it away how happy I am about what I'm having for dinner. I'm gonna remember the allergy story for other foster parents who might serve food I don't like.

I step outside the back door and see a massive cemetery behind the house. Derek and his brothers always said cemeteries were scary places, but the flowers on the stones are so pretty. What's so scary about flowers?

With my sandwich in hand, I skip over to check out the names on the stones. This is actually a super cool place to play. Maybe I can find a hiding place around here somewhere.

Right when I reach the first grave, the strawberry jelly slips out of my mouth and lands on my shirt and on the flowers on the ground. I try to clean it off the large, white flower. "I'm sorry to whoever you are. I didn't mean to make your flowers all dirty. I wonder if you're with Jesus." I edge closer to make out the writing on the stone.

Ralph, our little boy, rests here. Born 1968 to 1978.

Wow, this was a *kid*. I put my hand on his stone. "Hi, Ralph. Great to meet you. I'm sorry you had to die when you were ten years old. That's how old I am." I immediately feel sad, like a big blanket covers my entire body. I sit down next to Ralph's flowers, being careful not to crush them. That might make his parents sad if they come to visit him.

Does anything about me make Norma sad? Like giving me away?

"Sometimes, Ralph, I wish I were dead. If I could be with Jesus, I would be with the one person who truly loves me. I'm guessing you're together with him at the moment. Let Jesus know that Anna says *hi* if you're able to hear me." I take another bite of my sandwich. "I'm new around here. I live in the foster home right there." I point toward Georgia's house, and then I chuckle. "Sorry, Ralph. I forgot that you can't see where I'm pointing." I take another yummy bite. "Sometimes, I'd rather be dead than live this horrible life. It feels as though I have nobody and am completely alone. The only person I had in my life was my brother, Curtis, but my caseworker, Mrs. Alex, separated us during one of the foster homes before, and I'm completely clueless about what's happened to him since then."

My sandwich feels heavy at the bottom of my stomach.

"You must've been loved a lot because of all the flowers and toy fire truck around you." Only parents who truly loved their kid would leave so much by the grave. I don't have this much, and I'm living. I get closer, picking up the red fire truck. "Would it be all right if I play with this here?" Carefully, I move the rusted red truck around on the grass in front of me. "Being ten and all by myself, with no parents or anyone, is tough because you have no one to protect you. I'm sorry your parents lost you. Some parents don't want anything to do with their kids like me. And others who love their kids can lose them. That doesn't sound fair to me."

"Maybe I can clean this truck for you next time so it's not so dirty." I brush grass from the ladder, which is probably there from someone mowing. "Do you have any brothers or sisters? My new foster brothers don't seem nice at all, except for maybe the little one, Kevin. He did ask about me. The older boys, I'm not liking them much because they hit me in the face with a ball." I lay on the ground next to Ralph as I rub my face.

I begin to make faces out of the clouds. I think I see a tree. Then, the angel wings float in. It's surprising how many things you can find in the clouds when you're looking.

"All right, Ralph, I should leave now. This new foster mother is a mean lady and is already hitting me. I need to find a hiding place before I go back inside because I'm going to need it to get away from the people in this foster home.

"I'll come to chat with you as much as I can, so you'll always have someone to talk to."

As I go to grab my uneaten sandwich, I'm grossed out to see ants all over it. Eww, how am I going to pick that up? I can't stand ants, but I won't leave them here next to Ralph because his parents made this all pretty for him, and I don't want to ruin it. I grab the ant-infested sandwich and hurry toward the woods to throw it away.

I see something in the grass, then bend down to get a better look. Grass and leaves cover a stone step—actually, there are five steps altogether, leading somewhere. I would've never spotted them if I hadn't thrown away that sandwich.

I carefully grasp the sharp needles and attempt to push through them. Ouch. This isn't working. I pick up a stick and start hitting the bushes. I know how to win the battle with prickers as I have practice from my first foster home with Daddy. I had to walk through pricker bushes to get to my hiding place there, the sluice pipe fort. So, I got this.

I follow the steps through the horse nettles and find—

117

Oh, wow. It's an old, rundown, tall stone house. It could've been a small castle.

It's shaped like a small circle without any doors or windows in it and tall grass all around.

I'm about to go in, but then I realize that I don't know what snakes they have here. There could be rattlesnakes or copperheads, and while I'm good at catching snakes, I only do that with ones that don't have poison.

I pick up the stick I'd used to get through the prickers to check out the grass before I walk through it.

As I get closer, I see that the roof looks like it has fallen off, but the walls are still standing. I step inside. In the center, there's only a tall stone square and nothing more.

Moving into the castle, I stumble upon what appears to be a miniature stone stage. That's strange. I wonder why they had that in their castle. Did they put on plays? I picture kids like me singing and dancing in my mind. The song of a bird flying above me grabs my attention.

Standing on the stone stage, I notice a doorway that has plenty of sunlight shining through it. This is nothing like the secret dark tunnel at Momma Johnson's. As I walk into the room, I realize that half of the wall is gone, but an old fireplace is still standing.

I brush some leaves off it, but this whole place needs cleaning. I like it as a hiding spot—especially the fireplace—because no one is going to think to look for me here.

I can hear crows squawking as they fly overhead. The noises they make are completely different from those of singing birds. They seem to be flying in a circle. My Daddy told me that these black birds do this when they are waiting for something to die. I shiver at the thought. I'm sad, thinking of an animal lying somewhere and dying. I love animals and hate the idea of them being alone.

I hate that feeling. But I'm okay being alone in my hiding place if I have to be.

I walk over to the tall wildflowers that I see around the castle-like building and pick a few of them to leave on the stage so the boring gray stone walls have some color.

I had better get going; Georgia gets mad easily. I make my way back out through the tall grass and prickers. Before heading back to the cemetery, I double-check that none of the boys are out there searching for me.

"See you later, Ralph; it was nice speaking with you. I stumbled upon a fantastic hiding place where I doubt anyone can find me. I should leave now. Goodbye again." I rush back to the house, unsure of how much time has passed.

Georgia's sitting in the living room, watching television. "I wondered where you had gone." She takes a sip of her pop. "Have you finished unpacking your room?" She continues staring at the television, like I'm not important enough to waste her time on.

"Did you mean, did I unpack in the small room at the end of the hallway?" I raise my eyebrows. "I put my stuff on my bed. I didn't see a dresser to unpack my clothes. And—the room is not even big enough to put a dresser in it anyway."

"Are you being fresh?" She finally turns her head in my direction. There's a pain in my stomach whenever I lock eyes with her.

"That bedroom that *we made for you* used to be a hallway closet, and since we can't have you sleeping in the room with the boys, we did the best we could with what we have. You just need a space big enough for a bed, and since you'll only be there for sleeping, how big does it actually need to be?" She looks back at the television.

"Where do you want me to put my clothes, then?"

'Easy child. It sounds like you're giving me attitude, and trust me, you don't want to do that. Leave your clothes in the garbage bag and shove that under your bed. You can pull what you need out of it when you need it." Really, she wants me to live in my garbage bag. I shake my head.

"Can I have some soda? I drank it all the time at Momma Jays?"

"Sorry Anna, No. This is mine to drink only." Mother, she is Mother. We weren't allowed to dri—

"Hey, Mom, this soda is crap. Where did you buy it?" Brad walks into the room with a soda in his hand.

I tilt my head at Georgia. "Sorry, Anna. *You* can't have any pop. I don't get enough money to buy you anything extra like that." I make a fist, dig my nails into my skin, and glare at Georgia.

"Do you have something you'd like to say?" She leans over the armchair at me. There's a lot I'd like to say to this nasty witch. You're a nasty, mean ol' bag that should be alone for the rest of your life because you deserve to feel what that's like.

"Leave her alone, Mom. She's just a kid," Brad tells her.

"Mind your own business, Brad." She playfully slaps him as he walks by her.

Control your anger, Anna, and use your head. I let go of my fist.

"I'm going to my room now," I whisper.

She takes in a deep breath and then blows it out. "You don't need to announce your every move. Get going."

With every step I take up the stairs, I repeat in my head, *I hate that woman. I hate that woman. I hate that woman.*

As I walk by, I can hear the boys in the room playing a game or something. How horrible is this? My two least favorite rooms are right next to each other: the boy's room and the bathroom. I've been hurt in both of these in past foster homes. Is there anything about this house I could possibly like?

I stop by the bathroom to pee. Once inside, I look for a lock. Nothing. I can't lock the door because there's nothing on it. How will anyone know I'm inside if I can't lock it?

I pace back and forth in front of the toilet, crossing my knees and keeping an eye on the door. If I don't hurry, I'll end up peeing in my pants. I pee as fast as possible, never taking my eyes off the door.

Just as I finish buttoning up my pants, the sound of the boys talking reaches my ears. "Hey, Clay, what do you think about living with a girl? She's close to your age. You might finally have a girlfriend."

"Scott, leave Clay alone and pay attention. It's your turn to throw the dice." Did Brad come upstairs while I was in the bathroom? It sounds like him talking.

Girlfriend for Clay? What the heck did Scott mean by that? Are they talking about me? I become sick at the thought. No way will I become someone's girlfriend here. No way!

I sprint from the bathroom to my tiny room, then swiftly close the door which, like the bathroom, doesn't have a lock. There's no way for me to stop someone from getting into here!

That's not good.

There *is* a small chair against the wall, but it doesn't look big or strong enough to hold the door closed. But it's better than nothing. I take it and prop it backward under the doorknob, hoping it holds it shut.

"Anna, it's time to get ready for bed," Georgia says as she stands at my door. "And, putting this chair against the door is unnecessary. There's no reason to be concerned, as it clearly didn't stop me from opening the door just now." I'll wake you up early for breakfast before catching the bus. When I call, make sure to get up, and don't make me ask twice." She stands with her hands on her hips.

There's no chance I'll use the bathroom at nighttime. Who knows what the boys will do if she's sleeping? If I have to, I'll hold it for the entire night.

I slip into the bed, roll over, and snuggle with Teddy and Raggedy.

Jesus, I hope you are still here with me. I'm at a new place again, and this one doesn't feel so good. I know you wouldn't put me here on purpose. Maybe you thought she was a nice person. But she's not at all. And the boys that live here—scare me. Can you keep them away from me? I don't know about this place, Jesus, so I may be singing to you a lot. How's Momma doing? I know she must be sad. Can you take care of her? How's my brother Curtis? I wish I could talk with him. It's been a long time since I've seen him. Well, goodnight, Jesus, and I'll talk with you tomorrow. Amen.

Anna shut your eyes and act like you're sleeping.

Chapter 15
A Chair

I wake up to the sound of creaking. As I turn around, I notice someone standing in my doorway. I'm not sure who it is. Is it Scott? Is it Clay? The person is too tall to be Kevin and too short to be Georgia or her husband, Frank.

At times, I listen to my voice in my head, and sometimes I do the opposite. Tonight, I have a gut feeling that something is urging me to pay attention. I close my eyes and pretend to be sleeping. I breathe slowly, trying to stop my heart from beating so loudly. Soon enough, the person in my doorway walks away with each creaking step.

What the heck was that? I think they went into the bathroom. I wait till I hear them leave. I know Georgia says this chair won't hold the door closed, but at least I'll hear it move when someone tries to come into my room.

Finally, the person leaves the bathroom. I hear them stop by the boys' room. Why would Scott or Clay be standing in my doorway watching me sleep? I tiptoe to my bedroom door closing it. I place the chair tight against it. This will work. When the door opens the chair will fall backward. I make sure the back legs are the only ones on the ground.

I find it hard to fall asleep for the rest of the night.

My eyes jolt open when I hear Georgia scream and the chair crash to the floor. "What the hell is this? The darn chair just slammed into my shins when I opened your door." Though I'm half asleep, I still chuckle to myself. I thought she said the chair wouldn't work. Ha.

"Anna, wake up and get ready. I'll be waiting downstairs for breakfast and put this damn chair back against the wall." Georgia is definitely mad. Is she mad that she got hurt or that I was right about the chair? Either way, I feel good about either reason.

I don't lay out any clothes at night. I pick them out in the morning. Come to think of it, I don't ever remember Momma getting mad if I was late. I know she hated being late for anything, so maybe I just got used to being early and didn't know it. I do know that when she did my beads, she would mention what color to wear the next day for everything to match.

I sprint to the bathroom. To prevent the door from opening, I use the laundry basket as a blocker. While washing my hands, I notice my braids are a total mess, with hair sticking up all over the place when I glance in the mirror. I make the loose strands look better by wiping them down with water. It seems to work.

"Yo, Anna! Move it or lose it! The bathroom is calling my name!" Scott yells from the other side of the door. This kid said nothing to me all day yesterday, but today, he acts like we've been talking the entire time. Weird!

I open the door, and Scott does a little side-to-side step, which means I can't get past him.

"Can you move?" I'm not going to let him know this bothers me. Derek used to love making me mad, and then hurting me. I don't need another foster brother doing that to me, so I can't let him know it bothers me.

"Did you have a good sleep?" Scott's smile isn't nice—and he knows I know it. And, yet, he doesn't move.

"Can you get out of my way? I have to get ready." Derek used to love knowing he scared me; it's taught me something, and I'm not going to let Scott do that same thing to me.

"Certainly, Anna. I'll do *annnnything* for you."

I walk past him and—

What the heck? He *slapped* my butt!

Oh no. Not again. No one's going to hurt me *ever* again, and especially not in my girl parts.

I swing around and punch him in the shoulder as hard as I can.

Scott grabs my arm and glares at me. "You're going to be sorry for that," he spits out before shoving me backward. I stagger to stay on my feet. Scott laughs and turns his back to me as he goes into the bathroom.

I stomp my feet. That kid sucks. "I'm not afraid of you. And don't you *ever* touch me again!" I lied to him. I am afraid of him, but I won't tell him that. He whips around with his hand on the doorknob. "You should be." He slams the door in my face.

What does that mean? Whatever it is, it doesn't sound good. I'm glad I found that hiding place. I have to make sure to put that chair in place tonight before I fall asleep.

"Anna, get down here for school," Georgia yells up the stairs. What about Scott, who is still in the bathroom in his pajamas? Why isn't she yelling at him to get ready? I need to find a way to leave this house. Maybe I can figure out how to call Mrs. Alex. This is one time I wish I could see her nasty green monster car pull into the driveway.

"Okay, Georgia, I'll be right down." I open the garbage bag to find some clothes.

There's a letter from Momma Jay.

Oh, I miss her so much. I'd felt so safe with her, and now—

I open the envelope, hoping her words make me feel better because, right now, I want to go punch Scott in the face.

Chère, I'm so sorry. I tried to make the caseworker let y'all stay here with me. I found Patty in the garbage can when Mrs. Alex was packing up the room. I'll take care of her for y'all. Y'all the most wonderful girl and don't you forgets it. Youl grows up and be a good person. I'll always think about y'all. Mo linm twa."

As I utter, "Momma," my face becomes drenched with tears. I know that *mo linm twa* means *I love you*. How I loved her, too, and I miss her so much.

As I dress, I wipe off teardrops that fall on my shirt and pants. I'm finally ready, but holding back the tears is a battle. I can't go downstairs and let this new foster mother see me crying. I can't let her see me be weak. I have to be strong in front of her. No way. I keep taking deep breaths until they finally stop.

Just like at dinner, I'm the last person to sit down for breakfast. Momma used to make me all kinds of food before I left for school. She used to say, "De best way t'start de day is wida food and conversation." Instead of my favorite grits, pancakes, and eggs, though, here, it's cereal and a glass of juice.

"Well, don't just stand there and look at it," says Georgie. "Grab a seat and get yourself a bowl of cornflakes." She brushes a hand over my hair, then flips a braid. "This looks messy, which is exactly the reason white people shouldn't wear braids. I'll fix them tonight. I wanted to do it last night, but I was too tired to put all that work into your messy-looking hair." She flips another one, making the beads clack together, each one hurting my feelings because I *love* these braids—and especially the love and care, Momma, put into creating each one for me.

Georgia flicks another one, and I just want to punch her. But by the time I could turn around to do it, she'd be done torturing me with my braids.

Instead, I cross my arms. "I want them to stay in. I like them."

Georgia tugs one of them.

"Ouch." I try to move so she can't pull my hair.

She just does it harder. "I *said* that I'll take them out tonight, and that's what will happen, got it?"

I don't say a word. I'm not going to give her the satisfaction of hearing me beg for them.

I also don't want to cuss in her face. Daddy told me that was wrong, but it would sure feel good right now.

She yanks on the braid once more. "Did you hear me?"

"Yes." One word because I'm not giving her anymore.

"Good, and I'm glad we understand each other. Sit down and have your breakfast."

I do as she says, but I don't reach for any cereal. I'd rather go hungry than eat her gross food. I loved the smell of coffee at Momma's house, but here, it makes me feel sick.

"All of you, take your plates to the sink when you're done, then get outside for the bus. Have a good day, boys," Georgia bends and kisses Kevin's head, then hugs Scott and Clay as they walk by.

My bowl clangs against the bottom of the sink.

125

She turns in my direction. "Be careful with those dishes. They weren't cheap. Get out to the bus."

She glares at me as I walk by her.

The boys and I stand in line, waiting for the bus to arrive. "Anna, you can sit with me if you like." When I look down, I see Kevin, the youngest brother, who is in kindergarten. "Do you wanna sit with me on the bus?" He has a bigger head that doesn't match his small body and blond hair that resembles Curtis's a little. While we wait for the bus, he takes my hand.

"Sure, Kevin, I'll do it."

All of a sudden, Kevin bursts into tears.

I look at him. Scott's finger is in his ear, giving him a wet willy.

My eyes narrow, making it so the only thing I can see is Scott's face. I let go of Kevin and shove Scott to the ground.

Clay laughs. "Shut up, fatso." Scott barks at Clay. Clay may be a bit heavy, but he shouldn't be called "fatso" No one likes to be made fun of, and so far, Clay hasn't done anything to me. But then again, he hasn't talked to me either.

The bus finally shows up. Scott shoves me aside, and just as he steps onboard, he looks right at me. "Your time's coming. Be careful tonight." He sticks out his tongue.

I do it right back. This kid drives me crazy!

Clay and Scott head to the back of the bus while Kevin and I take the fourth seat.

"Who's that girl who hopped onto the bus with you all?" a voice calls out from the back, then he sings, "Clay has a girlfriend, Clay has a girlfriend!"

He hits the kid in the arm. "Shut up, or I'll punch you in the face."

"Scott, your new sister has a good set of front teeth on her." A kid in the back of the bus makes beaver sounds by making smacking noises with his mouth.

I know that sound because I've heard it my entire life. Kids are just as mean as adults sometimes. Are there any more nice people like Momma Jay, Daddy, or Jessica?

We finally pull up in front of the school.

The bus driver stands up, "Please hold on, everyone. We're going to do a drill and exit out the back of the bus this morning." He leaves the bus and pushes the door closed behind him.

Every single person yells and cheers. I've never seen this before—we always got out the front door, so I don't have any idea what's happening.

The rear door of the bus opens, and everyone, including the bus driver, screams, "Move it! Move it! There's a fire!"

Without hesitation, I seize Kevin's hand. "We have to get off the bus! There's a fire!"

I drag him out into the aisle and use the lever to open the front door. Kevin and I, followed by a few other kids, get off the bus.

"The new girl went out the front door!" a redhead girl shouts at the bus driver.

"Stay where you are!" The driver yells at me from the back of the bus.

People laugh as they pass me. I have no clue what is so funny, so I make a mad face at them. I'm so tired of people laughing or making fun of me.

Scott stops in front of me, "Stupid, the bus wasn't *really* on fire." And by the way, you're going to get it later when you get home for pushing me down. You wait." He grins and walks away into the gigantic school.

The bus driver walks over to us. "Kevin, go into the school. You know where to go."

Kevin drops my hand and then makes his way into the building.

Next, the driver looks at me. "What made you think it was acceptable to exit through the main door?"

I fold my arms and tilt my head up so I can see him. "Because you yelled that the bus was on fire, and I didn't want to wait in line with everyone else and burn up. So, I just opened the front door." I inhale because I'm frustrated. How did I know it was a drill? If someone yells fire, I'm getting out of wherever I am.

He laughs, which jiggles his belly. Hmmm. He seems happy, so I ask, "How was I supposed to know you were lying?"

"You've got a good point there, young lady." He stops on the first step and turns to study me for a second. "I understand that you're new here, and nobody likes to do things alone in the beginning. Well, you don't have to go through this alone, young lady. I'll go inside with you." We take a few steps, "I'm Paul. It's nice to meet you. I'm sure it's not easy being a foster child and moving from place to place and school to school." Paul sounds nice, but I don't know what he wants me to say or do.

"It's not." That's all that I want to say.

'Well, Anna, if anyone gives you a hard time on the bus, you can let me know." He put his hand up for a high-five.

I smack his hand. "Okay, I will."

It doesn't take long for us to reach the main office. "Allow me to introduce Anna Snow. It's her first day, and she just moved in with the Krays. Could someone please help her get settled and give her a tour?"

A lady resembling Momma with black skin smiles and steps out from behind the desk. "Your braids look amazing," she said, "and the beads are a nice touch. Did Georgia do this for you?"

I can't *not* laugh at *that* idea. "You've *got* to be kidding. She wants to take them out tonight because she doesn't like them. My last foster mom, Momma Jay, did them every night." I smile, feeling proud of my hair. She always made sure it looked pretty. I look down at the blue swirls on the floor and feel sad.

The office lady touches a few beads. "These braids are definitely done by someone skilled in the old ways of doing hair." She continues to touch a few more areas on my head. "Yup, these are tight. There's no mistaking it; a Black woman did this." She smiles as I look up at her.

"Momma is Black—Louisiana, French Creole." I smile as big as I can. I love to talk about Momma. Though I'm sad because I'm not with her, I feel happy talking about her. We did a lot of things together, even more than Daddy and I did. Though I lived with Daddy a lot longer than Momma Jay.

"Well, she sure did a great job. Time to get you to Mrs. Fran's class."

I walk behind her as we make our way down the hallway.

"Mrs. Fran."

A pretty teacher with long, black hair greets us as we walk into the classroom. She looks like a little kid herself.

Paul starts talking to her right away. "Allow me to introduce Anna Snow, your new student. She's living with Georgia and Frank Fray."

I cross my arms in front of me. *Please don't make me stand in the front and become part of a freak show like all the other teachers have done.*

Mrs. Fran leans in and whispers, "It's a pleasure to have you here, Anna. Take the seat behind the first one in the second row."

My seat is on the opposite side of the room from where the windows are located. Ugh, I need to figure out how to pass the time during math period.

"Anna Snow is now a part of our class—let's give her a big welcome!"

"Hi, Anna!" They all say it at once like they rehearsed it or something.

I wave but say nothing. I don't like everyone looking at me, and I don't like to talk in front of the class, which is why I hate reading aloud.

"Don't forget to write September 20th on all of your papers, class." Mrs. Fran writes the date on the board.

All teachers seem to do this same exact thing at the start of each morning. Why do we have to write the date down? What does it matter anyway?

It's only been a day since I was ripped from a woman who truly loved me. Mrs. Alex took away the only two parents, Daddy and Momma Johnson, who loved me—and I'm *not* calling them foster parents because they were like real parents to me. Why would Norma want me to leave Momma just because of the color of her skin? Why does Norma even care?

Maybe she didn't. Maybe Mrs. Alex lied because she didn't want me to be happy.

"Anna, would you like to write the answer on the board?"

I was so busy thinking that I didn't even know that we'd switched from reading to math.

"I'm sorry, but I'll pass."

The entire class bursts into laughter.

"Anna, that wasn't a question. I'd like you to write the solution on the board."

"Ah, nope. That actually *was* a question. You asked me if I wanted to write the answer on the board, and I said no."

Now, everyone goes quiet.

At first, Mrs. Fran looks mad. "Excellent work paying attention. You are completely right; it *was* a question." She giggles, but just a little bit. "Seventeen is the right solution."

Just as she finishes writing on the chalkboard, the recess bell rings. Racing outside, the kids in the hallway bump into each other, trying to get ahead.

Since I don't know anyone, I take my time.

129

"Anna, would you mind shutting the door on your way out since you're the last one to leave? Enjoy the outdoors." She goes back to the stack of papers in front of her. Why can't *she* stand up and shut the door? Does she expect her students to do all the work in her class? The last time a teacher asked me to do something, I walked to the office to see Mrs. Alex standing there to take me away again. I wasn't happy about it then, but I sure would be now.

It makes me think of Sue, my former foster mother because she was always asking me to get her drinks, snacks, and other items. Not to mention that horrible secret girl time. I shake my head because I don't want to think about that ever again. I wish I could erase it from my mind like I can erase my mistakes with my pencil.

As soon as I get to the playground, I'm looking for the kids that are jumping rope. So far that is a common thing at recess, and I hope that's the case with this school too. I move around trying to get a good look as there are a ton of kids at this school, and it looks like we all have recess together because it's hard to move around without running into someone.

Then I see the single rope spinning, and a line of girls is ready to jump. I walk fast to stand in the back of the line, waiting for my turn. Finally, I reach the top of the line, and a girl with long blonde hair steps in front of me.

"Hi, Anna." Do you want to join us? I'm Belinda, and this is my sister, Ashley. Our cousins Jacquelyn and Kristy, along with some of our other friends, are the ones turning the rope."

As soon as I dive in and start turning, the girls start screaming and clapping. Jumping rope is one thing I can do when no one cares about my teeth, hair, or clothes. It's the one place where people don't make fun of me and cheer me on. It seems like I just started to jump, and the bell goes off to return to class. The girls drop the ropes fast as I stand among them.

"Come on, Anna, you can walk with us. Jacquelyn takes my hand as we walk towards the school. "You're really good at jump rope."

"Thank you. I love to jump."

We start to skip together, and I pull my hand away. Why are people so touchy all the time?

We're back in class before recess even feels like it started. I didn't realize that Ashley and Kristy sat in front of me. Ashley passes me a note while we work on spelling. "Can you double dutch? Yes or no?" I circle the yes, tap her shoulder, and slide the note back into her hand. Am I making friends? Belinda, Ashley, Kristy, and Jacquelyn all seem so nice, and I don't think there's a mean girl in this school. Or at least I haven't seen one yet.

Ashley reaches back with the note in her hand. Carefully, I lean forward and take it.

"Good. Wanna be my partner tomorrow? You're good at jumping." She drew a smiley face. Again, I circled yes and sent the note back to her. We passed notes all day in class. She asked me questions about dancing and music while I asked her about her favorite things to do.

The bell rings for school to end, and for the first time, I don't want to go home. I had fun today, and I don't want it to end.

Once again, I choose to sit with Kevin on the way back to the foster home.

"Bye, Scott, have fun with your new sister!" one of the kids from the back of the bus yells as others laugh.

"Shut up, assholes!" he yells back.

What did the kid mean when he told Scott to have fun with his sister. Did Scott tell him what he planned to do to me today? Scott told me earlier I was going to *get it*. I wonder if the kids on the bus knows. Scott almost pushes me off the step as he jumps past me.

"Easy, Scott, you almost knocked Anna down the steps," Paul yelled. I don't think Scott heard him, as he was already on the porch and at the front door.

It's nice that Paul is looking out for me. I wish he could move into this house to do that.

When we walk in, Georgia's in the middle of preparing dinner. "How was your day at school? Do we have any homework to do tonight?"

We all say no at the same time.

I go upstairs to hang out with Teddy and Raggedy. I feel weird hanging out with the foster family downstairs. I don't feel like I'm one of them. I'd rather be in a place where I feel like I belong, and Raggedy and Teddy have always been with me. Raggedy longer than Teddy, of course.

Noisy crashes come from downstairs. I run down the steps to make sure the building isn't collapsing. The moment I step into the kitchen, I'm paralyzed with shock as I see a pile of smashed dishes on the floor, with no one around. Within seconds, Georgia is behind me, screaming at the top of her lungs.

"What the hell happened here? Who is responsible for throwing my fine china on the floor?" Her face, now red, shifts to me. "Did you do this?"

Scott bursts into the kitchen out of nowhere. "It was Anna, Mom. I saw her take the plates out of the cupboard and throw them all over the place. She said she was mad at you. I can't believe she did that, and I tried to stop her, but I was afraid she'd hurt me by throwing a plate at me."

I shout, "He's lying!"

Chapter 16
Please

Georgia runs across the kitchen screaming as she steps over all the broken dishes to reach me on the other side. She yanks my hair, so I face her. "Why would you do this? We welcome you in when nobody else does, and this is how you show your appreciation?" She yanks my head again as she pulls hard at my hair.

"I didn't do it! Scott's lying!" I shout so that she can hear me over Scott's yelling.

"Anna's lying, Mother! I saw her do it! After she threw them on the ground, she ran back up to her bedroom."

Georgia looks at Scott, who is sobbing and acting like a baby. With one hand on my hair, she pulls me toward her as she takes a step toward Scott, then runs her fingers through his hair. "I believe you. You've never lied to me before in fifteen years." She speaks to Scott in a soft, nice voice. "I'll be back to check on you after I take care of Anna."

Her eyes blaze as she turns her attention back to me. "I'll make sure you never forget this punishment and learn from your mistake, young lady."

I'm dragged by my hair to a small room connected to the living room.

"Anna's going into the beating room. She's in for it now." Clay's high-pitched voice follows me into the dark brown room.

Georgia slams the door shut, then whirls me around. "This is something you'll never forget." She grabs a large belt from a wall hook.

My heart pounds hard hurting my chest. "I can't breathe. Georgia, I can't breathe." It's like someone punched me in the ribs. "Believe me, Georgia, I'm telling the truth. I didn't do it. It wasn't me. I don't know who it was, but it wasn't me. Please don't hit me."

With the belt in her hand, Georgia pulls her arm back to swing it through the air.

I crouch down and cover my head with my hands for protection.

The leather whips across my back—a feeling I remember well from my first foster brother Derek.

As I continue to plead with Georgia, she strikes the back of my *head* with the belt

Pain shoots through my neck.

"Please stop!" I raise my hands in the air while crouching on the ground trying to protect my head.

The next swing lands across my lower back.

"You're hurting me!"

"That's my plan. This is a beating you will never forget," she growls, her voice full of hate.

I've got to get away from this woman!

I try to get to my feet, but the belt cracks across my legs.

"I didn't do it, Georgia! You have to believe me!"

She doesn't say anything; she just keeps hitting me, over and over.

I reach up to grab the belt mid swing so I can pull it from her. Georgia pushes my hand.

Nothing I'm doing is working. Nothing.

I give up trying to get away and curl up into a ball on the floor.

The blows keep coming.

I try to think of something to take me away from this horrible place. The sharp daggers of pain in my body remind me where I am and that there's no escape.

I know Jesus loves me, for the Bible tells me so. Little one to him below: They are weak, and he is strong. Yes, Jesus loves me. Yes, Jesus loves me, for the Bible tells me so.

After what feels like an eternity, she finally stops whipping me. "Now that should burn a hole in your brain and the next time you think about lying or throwing around dishes and blaming them on someone else."

"Georgia, I didn't do it." I muffle out while I lay curled up on the floor. "Scott threatened me on the bus—he did this. He said I'd get what's coming to me. He set this up!"

"You still want to lie about it and blame it on my innocent son. Are you kidding me? Why don't you plan to stay in this room for a while before you head to bed for the night with nothing to eat? Maybe then, you'll finally tell the truth and stop blaming Scott, who saw you do it." No matter what I say, she's not going to believe me.

She turns off the light and slams the door on the way out.

And honestly? I'm glad. At least I know no one can see me like this.

No one can see me cry.

I don't want to cry. I don't want that woman to have this kind of power over me, but, boy, she got me good. I'm really hurt.

Why do some people have to be so mean? Someone broke the dishes, but it absolutely wasn't me. Was it Scott? Clay? Brad wasn't in the house tonight, and Kevin definitely didn't do it because he couldn't reach the dish cabinet.

I have to get out of here and go to my room. It might not be a real bedroom, but it's better than a dark closet of belts.

I try to stand up—but, boy, my legs are weak, and they burn like they're on fire.

It's so dark in here. It's good that Curtis isn't here; he's scared of the dark.

I'm not exactly happy with it right now, either, honestly.

I run my hands along the wall until I find the doorknob, but I open it slowly in case Georgia's sitting out there, waiting to hurt me some more.

Or Scott is…

I'm finally outside the door, standing in the living room and heading toward the stairs. Slowly, I walk up, hoping no one hears me. Georgia is talking loudly, and I can hear everything she says. "You boys are the greatest things in my life. Scott, I really appreciate you cleaning up the mess while I was busy with Anna. Do you believe the child holds *you* responsible? I'm sorry, Scott, you were accused of doing something you didn't do. I know we need the money she brings in right now, But I can't put you through this. I might need to rethink this plan. Maybe foster care is not a good option."

Handle? What does Georgia mean by *handling the matter*?

Once I'm upstairs, I tiptoe to the bathroom to clean up.

Whoa. The image in the mirror shocks me.

Is that me? I lean closer to the mirror.

I see my eyes fill with tears and look away. I don't want to cry over that nasty woman and what she did to me. I don't want you to cry for me, as I have to be strong to figure out how to get outta here.

Slowly, I removed my pants so I could use the bathroom. I'm shocked at what I see.

My pants are ripped, and I have buttons missing on my shirt. Several belt marks and welts cover my legs. No wonder my legs are hurting me. I need to get moving, as I don't want to run into Scott or Georgia. Slowly, I walk from the bathroom to my bedroom and shut the door. I look around for the chair. It's gone. Georgia must've taken that chair out of my room. Great!

Suddenly, my head throbs intensely, as if it might burst. When I lean in to touch it, I notice the big bald area where Georgia yanked out some of my braids. I'm filled with anger, sadness, and other emotions I can't explain as I stand and look at my bruised and swollen body.

Jesus, why are you letting people beat me up? Can't you stop them? Or is that the devil making them do it? Aren't you stronger than him?

Suddenly, Scott flings open the bathroom door, hitting the wall with a loud crack. I'm too late.

Scott is standing right there.

I yank up my pants.

Boys and me and no clothes in bathrooms are *not* a good thing.

"It seems like someone roughed you up." He leans against the door frame with an awful grin on his face, then laughs. "Remember when I said I'd get back at you? Well, I did. And there's not a thing you can do about it." He slams the door.

Good. At least he's leaving me alone.

For now.

I seriously don't know how someone can be so mean. What did I ever do to him? I just *got* here.

Chapter 17
Ever Again

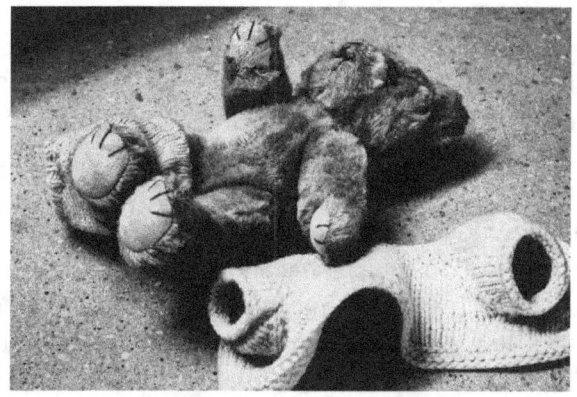

Georgia holds true to her threat of no dinner, but my stomach rumbles so loud that everyone downstairs might hear it—which will probably just get me in more trouble.

"Goodnight, Mom." I hear the boys' voices as they come upstairs, go to the bathroom, and then go to bed.

"Anna got her ass kicked today." Scott brags. I've come to learn his voice quite well.

"She sure did. Mom sounded like she was going crazy on her." Clay giggles as he walks down the hallway.

Soon enough, everyone is asleep in their rooms, and the lights are turned off for the night. I can't do anything else but focus on food because my stomach hurts from hunger.

Hello Jesus. Anna here. I'm not doing so good tonight. Georgia beat me pretty hard, and my body hurts everywhere. Can you help it feel better so it doesn't hurt when I walk? I know I've never asked this of you before, Jesus, but could you have Mrs. Alex show up and take me away from here? I don't want to live here anymore, please.

***

I'm sinking deeper and deeper into a swimming pool. People just stand around the edge, and no one is helping me as I sink to the bottom. Why aren't they doing anything to save me? I struggle to move my hands in the water, but I can't. The water's too heavy or something.

And then... I can't breathe—

I wake up.

There's a hand over my nose and mouth.

I can't move my legs.

"Hold her down, Clay."

Scott looms over me. "If you move or scream, I'll break something else so you'll get another beating. And if you thought today was bad, wait'll you see what she does over something really big?

"Gmmt... ommm... meeee..." I scream against his hand.

I'd rather get a beating than what he's planning to do.

I can't let him do this. I can't go through it again.

I wiggle my head to catch some air to breathe.

He whispers in my ear, "I mean it, Anna, don't move or make a sound. If you do, and Mom comes in here, I'll tell her that you were trying to hurt Clay. Who do you think she's going to believe?" Then he lies right on top of me all the way.

He's not wearing anything.

And neither am I.

Well, my nightgown is bunched up around my neck... but that's it. I don't have any underwear on.

Oh, no. Please. Not again.

"Clay, hold her legs open, "he whispers loudly. "This won't take too long.'"

And then he does to me the same thing Derek did, and it hurts, and I don't want this, and the room starts spinning, and his hand tightens on my mouth—that same disgusting sweat smell Derek had—and he's breathing in my ear so it's all I can hear, and he's moving up and down on me, and it hurts... It just... hurts.

And then he moves faster.

Oh, gross, the smell. This horrible, sweaty, gross-boy smell.

Salty blood fills my mouth as my teeth rip my lips open.

I feel the *whoosh* of air from his mouth as he tries to whisper to me, but I can't hear anything now. It's like my body isn't working anymore. I can't even move my head when he finally takes his hand off my mouth. I just keep staring at the ceiling.

Scott's face is right in mine, and his breath is just gross.

I stare at him as if he isn't real—and I wish he wasn't the pig.

"If you mention *anything* about what happened here tonight, I'll make sure you get the worst beating you've ever had in your life."

He climbs off me, and I can finally breathe again.

But I don't take a big breath because I don't want him to know what he did to me.

And how could Clay just stand there and *help* him? What is *wrong* with the people in this family? Does *anyone* here know how to treat another person?

I can't move—and I don't want to. I just want to float away and forget this ever happened, but—

He could come back. And what if *Clay* wants a turn?

Anna, get up! Move! At the very least, you need to go get cleaned up because you peed yourself on top of everything else.

I sit up—and a bolt of lightning shoots through my girl parts.

I just wanna go to sleep and forget this ever happened.

Take a deep breath, Anna. You must *move. What if he comes back? You* have *to move!*

Taking my time, I lower my nightgown and look around to find my underwear to put back on. Then I get on my feet.

One step at a time.

I make it to the bathroom. When I pee, it feels like a bee is stinging me *down there*. And there's blood—not a lot, but enough to remind me it really *did* happen.

Again.

I finish on the toilet, then look in the mirror.

I'm dirty.

Again.

I scrub my arms, legs, hands, and face with a washcloth, hoping the harsh fabric will get the feeling of Scott off of me.

I still feel dirty.

I head downstairs, my plan to hide from Scott fully formed. He's *not* going to do that to me ever again.

139

Chapter 18
Braids

If Georgia had told me I'd gladly walk back into this room on my own, I would have laughed at her. I would have spit in her face, honestly—well, I'd *want* to spit in her face, but her damn belt would make me not do it.

But, yeah, I'm going back in *that* room—it's the *last* place any of them will think I'd go, so I should be safe.

I open the door, slip inside, close it, then turn on the light.

The smell of leather is everywhere. Oh my gosh! E*very inch* of the walls is covered in *belts*. Some are wide, and others look like ropes. What on *earth* is this place? Why would anyone ever have a room like this in their house?

There's a sound from upstairs—is it Scott? Is he going back to my room?

I rush over to the light switch. I have to turn it off if I don't want him to find me here. My body shaking everywhere slows me down. I have to get to the light.

I feel along the walls to head toward a back corner. I slide down to the floor and then wrap my arms around my knees.

The darkness can't hurt me. The darkness can't hurt me.

I close my eyes so I don't have to see the darkness. I try not to cry, too, because I don't want anyone to hear me. Georgia would be furious to find me here—and might beat me again.

No, I have to be quiet if I don't want to get hurt.

I slide my hand to my girl parts—they *still* hurt. Why did Scott do that? And, actually, *how* did he do that? It was sort of like what Derek did, but Scott didn't use his finger because one of his hands was on my mouth, and the other was on the bed next to me. I don't know what he did, but I know that it hurt like crazy and still does. Why do boys do that to girls?

I hate it—I absolutely hate it—and nobody will ever do that to me again if I can help it.

But I couldn't help it with Scott.

What if he wants to do it again?

I can't stay here. I have to get out.

But if I go back to my room now, Scott could come back to the room and hurt me again.

Stay still, Anna.

Yes, that's what I'll do. I'll stay here until I hear them talking in the kitchen in the morning. Then I'll go to my room while they're eating and get all my stuff. I wish only Momma or Daddy was here. Why did Mrs. Alex have to take me from Momma?

I'm all alone.

There's no one else in this world with me.

I'm alone with people hurting me whenever they want.

I'm alo—

Sing to me, Anna.

Wait. What? Who's saying that?

It must be Jesus. My church teacher told me he'd always be with me.

Okay, Jesus, I'll sing to you.

Jesus loves me this I know,

for the Bible tells me so.

Little ones to him belong.

They are weak,

but he is strong.

Yes, Jesus loves me.

Yes, Jesus loves me!

Yes, Jesus loves me!
The Bible tells me so.
That church teacher was right; Jesus *is* with me when I need him, and he *does* love me.

Maybe I can get out of here after all.

***

"Where the *hell* is Anna?" Georgia's voice shatters the silence in a roomy hiding place, startling me awake.

I get to my feet and feel my way back to the door. Just about to turn on the light when I stop. What if she notices the light coming from under the door? I'll get in trouble for sure.

I have to avoid that at all costs.

"Get moving and search for her! Don't just stand around; she has to be *somewhere* in this house!"

Georgia sounds pissed, and I think she's standing right outside the door, so I don't move. I don't like the dark, but I don't like her and her belt more.

"Scott," she says, "have you come across Anna?" Oh, he has, the mean jerk. But he's not going to tell her that. And if I try to, she's never going to believe me.

Scott clears his throat. "No, I haven't."

Liar, liar, pants on fire!

Which mine seem to be—well, if I had pants. But my underpants area still feels like it's on fire after what he did to me. I want to throw up.

Oh no—I actually *am* going to throw up. How am I supposed to do that and be quiet?

No clue, but I just… do. Somehow, my body just pukes all over the place without a sound. I don't know how I do it, but I just do it, and now there's gross puke somewhere in this room.

Good. Serves Georgia right.

I wipe my mouth clean with the sleeve of my nightgown, then lean against the wall to wait.

"Frank, I have *no* idea where the hell she is. We've all checked everywhere. Based on her messy bed, it seems like she slept in it. Before I call the caseworker, I could use your help. Can you come home, please? She's quiet for a few seconds. Then she slams down the phone.

142

Frank must have said no, I guess.

Good, one less person I have to hide from.

"Anna, where the *hell* are you?" Georgia mumbles some more but I can't make out what she says.

"Morning. We can't find Anna. How far out are you? Okay, sounds good. Well, we might have to call the police in, as I'm not sure where she…" Georgia's voice fades as I lock in the final details of my plan to get outta here. If she's talking to Mrs. Alex, then Mrs. Alex will have to come here to look for me. Perfect. I need to have my stuff ready to go. I didn't realize that she hung up the phone till I heard dishes clunking in the kitchen.

I need to go now or never.

The intense brightness in the living room startles me, causing me to quickly close my eyes. *Move it Anna, you don't have time to think right now. Move it!*

I tiptoe up the stairs and head back to my room. Like a movie, the images from last night race through my mind as soon as I see my bed. His smell burns my nose. I cross my arms in front of me.

Come on Anna. Mrs. Alex is on her way to visit. I keep reminding myself. *Get your stuff together so this way when she comes in, you can leave with her whether or not she likes it.*

We're about to leave, Raggedy and Teddy. We just need to wait for Mrs. Alex to get here.

"Anna? Girl, where on earth *are* you?" Georgia sounds like she's… *right outside my door!*

Oh, no!

I jump off the bed, then slide underneath to hide from her.

Yep, sure enough, the door opens, and I see her old-lady-looking shoes come into the room.

"Well," she mutters, "one thing I can say about that girl—she never unpacked her stuff. That'll make this easy." I hear her open the garbage bag and go through it.

She has no right to do that! That's *my* stuff—all I have in the world!

"Well, look it here. Poor kid's trying to be Black." She shakes my box of beads from Momma. "That girl needs to act like a white girl. She doesn't need these."

I see her pat her pocket as she leaves the room.

She took my beads. The one thing I had from Momma Johnson, and now they're gone. How dare she take them?

I want to go after her and get them back, but I have to wait for Mrs. Alex to get here. I don't want to give Georgia any chance to call Mrs. Alex and tell her not to come. I *am* leaving this house, and I'm *not* taking *no* for an answer.

I slide out from under the bed, getting ready to get out of there as soon as Mrs. Alex's ugly green car shows up. I wish I had a window in this room that faced the driveway.

But then I hear a knock on the front door.

Georgia opens it. "Oh, thank goodness you're here."

I tiptoe out of the closet, which they call a bedroom, and peer around the corner to see who's here.

"Hello, we're here to help you find Anna Snow." It's a policewoman—

And Mrs. Alex is right behind her on the porch.

Just what I'm waiting for. I walk back to my room to grab my garbage bag, Teddy and Raggedy. I'm not leaving here without them. No one is taking *them* from me.

"When was the last time you saw her?" The police lady asks Georgia.

"She—"

I time my entrance perfectly. Everyone turns to stare at me as my garbage bag *clunks* its way down the stairs.

"Where the heck *were* you all night?" Georgia plays with her hair, using a much nicer tone than I've heard from her since I got here.

I stop in front of her. "I don't knows what y'all means. Ida been in de room all de night."

She glares at me with a confused look on her face. "What the he—"

"Goodbye, Georgia." I don't let her finish her sentence because, this time, I am getting the last word. "Your son, Scott, sucks. And he lies. He's the one who broke your dishes."

I stand in front of Mrs. Alex. "I'm leaving here no matter what you say, so open the door to your green beast and get me outta here now!" I walk onto the front porch to wait for her because there's no way I'm going back into that house.

Mrs. Alex ignores me and talks to Georgia. Ha! If she only knew about the beating room, I bet she wouldn't be talking so nice.

For a minute, I think about telling her, but that's gonna take too long 'cause Georgia will say I'm lying, and then I'll have to convince Mrs.

Alex and the police lady that the room exists. The last time I told Mrs. Alex about Mrs. Dorsey punching me, she didn't believe me and told me I made it up. So, what makes me think she'd ever believe me about the beating room or what Scott did to me last night? She'd say that I accused... And then they might not even believe me enough to go check it out, and, frankly, I don't care that much. I don't want to be here any longer than I have to be, which, in my mind, was twenty-four hours ago.

"Mrs. Alex, can we leave? I'm hungry and want a few of those fries you always buy on the trips."

"All right, Anna." She smiles at me—a first.

It works like I knew it would. Mrs. Alex can't resist those stupid fries. Kinda sad, really, but I don't roll my eyes because I want to get out of here.

"Let's head out, then." She waves to the monster she'd left me with. "Thank you, Georgia. I'll be in touch." She sweeps a hand toward her ugly car like it's a limo. "Let's go get you some of those delicious fries, Ms. Anna Snow."

She opens the door for me, and, for the first time, I'm happy to get in her car. While she's saying something to the police lady, I lean out the door and at Georgia, "Oh, by the way—there's puke and pee in your beating room!" I smile at her frowning face and slam the door shut. *Let's go, green beast. Get me out of this hellhole.*

Mrs. Alex finally shuts up, and the policewoman goes back to her car. "Can we go now, please? I'm hungry." I didn't like to lie to Momma because I loved her and felt bad. I can't say the same thing about Mrs. Alex. Lying comes easy with her.

"Anna, where were you last night, and why were you all ready to go this morning." I want to tell her because I used my smarts as Momma taught me. But instead, I lie. "I don'tcha know what you are talking about. I was in my room all night." I feel my smile spread clear across my face. This feels good. No one knows where I was. And—my plan worked to get out of there. I clap my hands together loudly, just like Momma did when she was happy.

"Anna, what was that? You made me jump while I'm trying to drive the car."

"I clapped my hands together because I'm happy about getting French fires, is all."

"Anna I'll ask again. Where were you hiding last night? Georgia said she checked your bedroom, and you were not there." That is a lie for sure. If Georgia would have checked the bedroom last night, she could have saved me from Scott.

"Georgia is a liar, and I don't want to talk about it anymore." I bury my head into my big, fluffy, and comfortable Teddy.

It doesn't take us long to get to the fry place.

"So, kiddo, do you really want some fries?"

"Mrs. Alex, can I go back to Momma's house? I liked it there, and she was really nice to me."

"I'm sorry, Anna, that cannot happen. Norma doesn't want you living with Maude Johnson."

"Why does Norma get to say where I live? She doesn't even want me, and I don't even know her."

"Because she's still your mother. That's why she can."

"No, she's not my mother. She's Norma."

I wipe a tear from my eye fast before she gets out of the car. I really don't want to eat anything, but this time, I'm happy that Mrs. Alex showed up when she did.

"Yeah. I'll take some fries."

She leaves the car, humming some song I've never heard before.

When Curtis left me and Mrs. Alex moved him to a new family, he used the sketchbook and crayons she left on the floor in the back seat to write me a note. I haven't found one since. If Mrs. Alex moved him, Curtis would definitely leave a note like he did the last time. If there is no note tucked in the seat, then maybe he is with the same family and not moving around like me.

Now's my time to look. I check all the cracks in the backseat, and there is…

Nothing.

But maybe I can leave one for him.

I grab the notebook off the floor with a crayon.

Dear Curtis,

I hope you are not moving as much as me and that's why there's no note from you. So, I thought that I'd leave you a note in case you're looking, too. I miss you, and I hope you are happy.

Love, your sister Anna.

I fold the note small enough to tuck into the crack in the back seat.

"What are you doing?" Mrs. Alex's voice makes me pull my hand out quickly. She opens the rear door and hands me a bag full of fries, smiling at me. She's happy.

I don't like her anymore when she smiles than when she is her normal self and doesn't. But I do say, "Thank you." She got me out of that nasty place, after all.

"We have a little ride ahead of us," she says as she gets back into her seat. "Enjoy the fries!"

I grab a fry and stare at it. I'd sworn I'd never eat any food she gave me, but since I'm starving from not having any food last night or this morning, I try it.

Ohmygosh, it's amazing.

"Anna, how did you know I was coming to move you? If Georgia couldn't find you to tell you to get packed?" She looks at me in the rear-view mirror.

"I didn't know you were coming; I wanted to leave that place. So I packed my stuff and decided to leave when you got there." I look back in the mirror at her.

"No, Anna. That's not what happened. I had to remove you because you broke her dishes. We can't have you act like that in anyone's home."

"But I didn't break them; Scott did." And he did a few other things, too… But I can't tell her that—I don't want her to think I'm dirty because then no one will want me. I mean, I had Momma Johnson and Daddy love me; there *has* to be someone else who will.

Right?

"And then there's your tendency to lie, Anna. You really must stop that."

No one ever believes me. *Never*. "But I'm not lying. Scott really did break the dishes."

"That's not what Georgia said, Anna. Why would you break all her dishes?"

"I! Didn't! Do! It! *Scott* did it and blamed me!" I feel the heat build up in my body.

"Anna, you must stop this lying. Lying won't get you anywhere, and foster parents will want you to leave—just like Mrs. Dorsey did. You accused her of punching you in the face, but there was no evidence to support it." This is why I didn't tell her about the beating room. I knew this is what she would do… call me a liar.

"Sure, there was. The other girls saw her do it."

"None of them corroborated your story, Anna."

"That's because they're all scared of her. They won't go against her. But I'm not lying!"

"Anna, it's time for you to quit telling your stories. Nobody is going to have faith in what you say. Can you explain why you broke the dishes?"

"I! Didn't! Break! The! Dishes!"

"Anna, that's enough. I'm unable to drive if you continue yelling."

I squeeze my hands together to make a fist. I don't lie. Why does she think that I do? I'm telling her the truth.

But, honestly, this doesn't surprise me at all. Mrs. Alex isn't nice, even though I'd hoped she would be. She just wants to believe everyone else over me.

She didn't believe me about Mrs. Dorsey and she doesn't believe me about the dishes. There's no *way* she would believe me about what Derek or Scott did to me. Or that Georgia took me into her beating room. She'd never believe me about that. I'm so mad. I don't even know *what* to do. I'm trapped in the car with her and can't get out until she takes me to whatever place she's gonna take me to.

And I don't want to go.

Why can't I just go back to Momma Johnson's? I was happy there.

My head itches where Georgia ripped out my hair. Mrs. Alex didn't even notice *that*. Maybe I should take out these braids so no one can see my bald spot.

"Anna, I'm just trying to help you."

What? That doesn't make any sense. How is she helping me by calling me a liar? She's not!

"Shut up, Mrs. Alex. I don't want to talk to you anymore."

I find myself playing with my braids to help me feel better. But at the same time, they make me feel sad as they remind me of Momma. Mrs. Alex says I can't go back to her so who will take care of my hair.

Slowly I remove the rubber band and take off the purple beads she put in my hair the last night I was with her. I untwist my hair so the braid disappears. Goodbye Momma. Thank you for loving me. I will miss you.

One by one, I remove the braids till…

… they are all gone.

About the Author

Dr. Sharon Zaffarese-Dippold's writing comes from her own lived experiences as a child who experienced multiple foster care and family placement moves involving all forms of childhood abuse and trauma.

Dr. Dippold attended approximately ten or more schools during her formative years as she moved from place to place. In spite of that, she earned a Bachelor in Social Work, a Masters in Social Work, and earned her PhD in Human Services from Capella University with a concentration in Human Behavior/Counseling Studies.

Her Doctoral Dissertation was published in 2016, The Lived Experience Of Former Foster Children Who Had to Move Their Belongings In Garbage Bags. A public speaker and trainer on foster care topics related to her story, her experience with bullying led her to create "INAM- It's Not About Me," an anti-bullying program that she presents in the school systems to deflect the impact of being bullied on children.

Dr. Zaffarese-Dippold lives in Saint Mary's, Pennsylvania, with her husband, where she enjoys spending time with her children and grand-children.

For motivational speaking, book signings, or training events, please contact Dr.Dippold@gmail.com or ZeeTPublishing@gmail.com.

Next in the series…

A Foster Care Story
Based on True Events.

JUST
another
DOOR

DR. SHARON ZAFFARESE-DIPPOLD

5
Garbage Bag
Life

www.ingramcontent.com/pod-product-compliance
Lightning Source LLC
Chambersburg PA
CBHW070709130626
46553CB00005B/1912